BFI Film Classics

The BFI Film Classics series introduces, interprets and celebrates landmarks of world cinema. Each volume offers an argument for the film's 'classic' status, together with discussion of its production and reception history, its place within a genre or national cinema, an account of its technical and aesthetic importance, and in many cases, the author's personal response to the film.

For a full list of titles in the series, please visit https://www.bloomsbury.com/uk/series/bfi-film-classics/

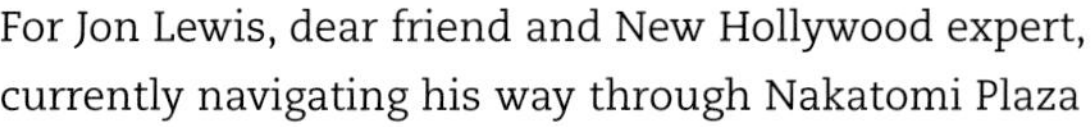

For Jon Lewis, dear friend and New Hollywood expert,
currently navigating his way through Nakatomi Plaza

'I am a lineman for the county / And I drive the main road / Searchin' in the sun for another overload'

'Wichita Lineman' (1968 hit song, lyrics by Jimmy Webb)

'More of a movie than it is a film, really'

Steven Spielberg describing *Close Encounters of the Third Kind*[1]

Close Encounters of the Third Kind

Dana Polan

THE BRITISH FILM INSTITUTE
Bloomsbury Publishing Plc
50 Bedford Square, London, WC1B 3DP, UK
1385 Broadway, New York, NY 10018, USA
29 Earlsfort Terrace, Dublin 2, Ireland

BLOOMSBURY is a trademark of Bloomsbury Publishing Plc

First published in Great Britain 2024 by Bloomsbury on behalf of the
British Film Institute
21 Stephen Street, London W1T 1LN
www.bfi.org.uk

The BFI is a cultural charity, a National Lottery distributor, and the UK's lead organisation for film and the moving image. We believe society needs stories. Film, television and the moving image bring them to life, helping us to connect and understand each other better. We share the stories of yesterday, search for the stories of today, and shape the stories of tomorrow.

Cover artwork: © Beatriz Martin
Series cover design: Louise Dugdale
Series text design: Ketchup/SE14
Images from *Close Encounters of the Third Kind* (Steven Spielberg, 1977), © Columbia Pictures Industries, Inc.
Film stills courtesy BFI National Archive
Additional image credits are listed on p. 100
'Wichita Lineman', words and music by Jimmy Webb. Copyright © 1968 UNIVERSAL – POLYGRAM INTERNATIONAL PUBLISHING, INC. Copyright renewed. All rights reserved. Used by permission. Reprinted by permission of Hal Leonard LLC

A catalogue record for this book is available from the British Library.

A catalog record for this book is available from the Library of Congress.

ISBN: PB: 978-1-8390-2577-8
ePDF: 978-1-8390-2579-2
ePUB: 978-1-8390-2578-5

Produced for Bloomsbury Publishing Plc by Sophie Contento
Printed and bound in India

To find out more about our authors and books visit www.bloomsbury.com
and sign up for our newsletters.

Contents

Acknowledgments

Greatest thanks to writer Paul Schrader and producer Michael Phillips for phone conversations about their efforts on *Close Encounters*. Zack Bendiner and Avery Gilbert hosted a screening with insight-filled neighbourhood kids Clem, Moses, Henry and Wyatt. Eleven-year-old Holden Daly-Castilla offered additional thoughts from a first-time viewing at NYU. Additionally, Kathy and Andrew Sheppard hosted a screening/discussion, and Kathy used her renowned jigsaw skills for the *Close Encounters* tie-in puzzle. Doctoral candidate Ryan Banfi employed his pinball expertise to research the *Close Encounters* machine. Cinephile-scholar Harvey O'Brien organised for me a *Close Encounters* lecture at University College Dublin (with a screening in their lovely cinematheque – appreciation to Catherine O'Brien for useful post-screening chat). My friend Noah Isenberg introduced me to Ryan Briggs, a University of Texas Ph.D. student, for research in Paul Schrader's papers in the university's archives. Hilary Swett at the Writers Guild of America obtained several *Close Encounters* scripts by Steven Spielberg himself. Jon Lewis and Caryl Flinn enabled ongoing email support, and Jon provided insight about Seventies cinema, as did Peter Krämer, *the* scholarly expert on the decade's blockbusters. Ray Morton, author of the *best* study of the making of *Close Encounters*, graciously advised on my own take on the film and offered supportive reading of the manuscript. By email, Dolby scholars Gianluca Sergi, Jay Beck and Mark Kerins provided useful explanations of the process. My appreciation to scholar-friends Tom Kemper, Blair Davis, Julie Turnock, Bradley Schauer, Sharrona Pearl and Keir Keightley for insights (some providing careful readings of the full manuscript), along with Dan North, Joshua Handler and Sam Kellogg for additional thoughts. Thanks to Lisa Gitelman for good conversation over early morning walks with wonder-dog Hudson. My gratitude to the engaged undergraduates in my intensive January-term course on *Close Encounters*. As the following pages confirm, Ken Sweeney's and Trevor Davis's accounts of their first viewings of *Close Encounters* (Ken's from opening week, 1977) capture the initial and *ongoing* appeal of the movie. Liza Greenfield offered detailed input on a draft manuscript and Gordon Leary discussed their first-time viewing impressions. Thanks also to Rochelle Miller and Joseph Fuller for additional reads (and helpful background bibliography/filmography from Joseph). As with my last two books, Genevieve Havemeyer-King, from NYU's Moving Image Archiving and Preservation Program, employed her talents to craft wonderful illustrations that capture here just how good-looking *Close Encounters* is. (At the last minute, another MIAP student, José Solé, helped with additional images for the book.) I offer my gratitude to the BFI team, Rebecca Barden, Veidehi Hans, Sophie Contento and ace copy editor Philippa Hudson.

As always, my immediate family, Marita Sturken and Leo Polan, provided loving support throughout this project.

Close Encounters of the Third Kind

Overture

When *Close Encounters of the Third Kind* (1977) was in production and then in box-office smash release, interviewers overwhelmingly would ask Steven Spielberg a predictable, perhaps too literal question – one that forgot cinematic form and instead emphasised content. Did he, they wondered, believe in UFOs? (Depending on the moment, he might answer Yes; sometimes he would declare himself 'agnostic'.) Likely, the question was beside the point: what did it matter whether the director offered belief in his movie's fantastic content? The more pertinent, never-asked question – maybe because the answer was visible right up there on the screen – was: did Spielberg believe in cinema? *Close Encounters* (as I'll shorten its name) is an ode to the power of moving images to inspire awe – not only for characters within its narrative but we spectators as the movie's sights and sounds wash over us hypnotically, spectacularly. (Sound needs to be insisted on, as the movie, we'll see, was destined early on for Dolby immersive multi-track audio.)

The following pages take as their central gambit to argue that within Seventies cinema, *Close Encounters* is not fundamentally a movie about alien spaceships per se but above all *about cinema itself* as an affective force and, here, it's obvious that Spielberg is a true believer. It's a movie movie – content matching form to enact cinematic seduction and display the deep affective powers of an emergent mode of blockbuster cinema.

In this respect, the following pages concentrate on the cinematic contexts for *Close Encounters* – other movies by Spielberg; other movies of the times; fan celebration, focused often on recondite technical aspects of the movie's making; critical appreciation (and dissension); tie-ins and franchising – along with filmic aspects internal

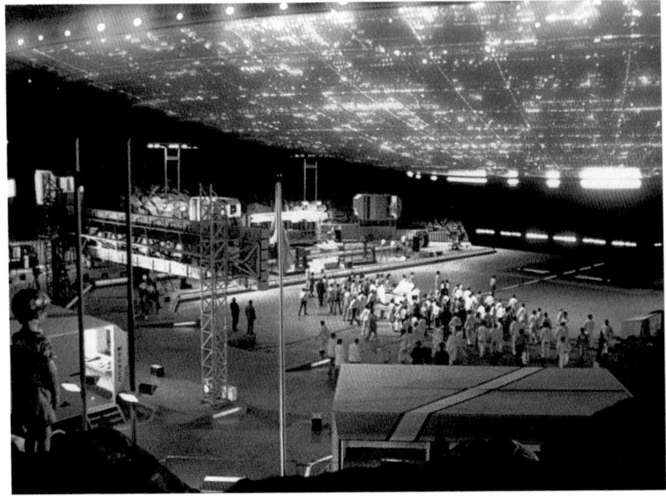

A movie movie

to the movie, such as the role of enveloping sound; the fascination with looking with awe at powerful events; the inscription, within the narrative, of acts of appreciation of spectacle, such as applause, that are then shared between character and audience alike; and so on.

Plot

As a reminder, *Close Encounters* chronicles how the luminous sighting that suburbanite Roy Neary (Richard Dreyfuss) has of UFOs becomes an inchoate obsession that impels him to journey to where government and scientists are preparing secretly for full encounter with extraterrestrials. Roy abandons spouse and children on his quest, yet he partners for a while with single mom Jillian Guiler (Melinda Dillon), whose son was spirited away during another alien visitation. Along the way, Roy and Jillian confront obstruction and obfuscation from the military, which wants to keep alien visitation under wraps, but ultimately the couple reaches the landing site constructed to greet the aliens. Jillian reunites with her son who emerges from the flying saucer. Head scientist Claude Lacombe (François Truffaut) sees that Neary needs existentially to participate in the mission and gives his blessing for Roy to join a team of astronauts trained to accompany the aliens back into outer space. Yet when the aliens arrive, they single out Roy and take him into their spaceship. (Even freezing the image doesn't clarify whether the expert space travellers enter the spaceship with Roy or not.) Ultimately leaving Jillian behind, Roy Neary heads off towards a seemingly wondrous future.

Setting the scene: a study in modern American culture

In the 1920s, sociologists Helen and Robert Lynd moved to what was, by all accounts, an average Midwestern town for on-site observation of the effects of modernisation on ordinary American traditions. The resultant book (1929) became a classic ethnography of everyday life, spawning numerous follow-up studies, even a public television series in the 1980s. To emphasise the generic quality of small-city life, the Lynds named their volume *Middletown* (subtitled *A Study in Modern American Culture*, with a sequel, *Middletown in Transition* [1937]), but word soon got out (including from the town's inhabitants) that 'Middletown' was a stand-in for the actual town of Muncie, Indiana.

The tradition of writings on 'Middletown' (including in the popular press), as well as fiction- and non-fiction films, has rendered Muncie an ongoing symbol of small-town Americana. It is, for instance, where hapless protagonist Norville Barnes (Tim Robbins) hails from in 1994's *Hudsucker Proxy* and which venal New York-bred Amy Archer (Jennifer Jason Leigh) herself claims as her folksy hometown in her scheme to exploit Norville.

I think it matters in this respect that as *Close Encounters* opens, Jillian Guiler and Roy Neary are each living, as a title declares, in 'Muncie, Indiana'. (The title comes up over Jillian's farmhouse but it's Roy who's living in *suburban* Muncie, and the film resolutely becomes *his* story as soon as he comes on screen.)

Middle America

Muncie, Indiana, is where Roy has an average American home, an average American family, an average American job and average American prospects. These all symbolise to him, even before his alien encounter, the dead ends of conventional existence. Once he's dazzled by the incandescence of the UFOs (a brightness so strong it actually burns half his face), Roy turns his back on family, home and job, and sets off in search of transcendent meaning.

In *Middletown*, the Lynds argued that close-knit Middle American traditions of church, schooling and family were unravelling under modernity's seductions. Radio was beaming into the home to broadcast opportunities beyond domesticity, the automobile enabled liberating movement away from that home life, and *the movies* visualised escape from home via dazzling promise of new worlds beyond a Middle American solidity and stolidity that increasingly seemed suffocating and stultifying, rather than inspiring.

I'd like to believe that the Middletown reference in the choice of Muncie as the starting point for (male) adventure in *Close Encounters* was intentional, but we can't be sure. For what it's worth, the film's co-producer Michael Phillips told me in conversation that he didn't remember how 'Muncie' was chosen but felt it resonated Middle Americanness. Whatever the case, in depicting conventional American life assailed by modernity, *Close Encounters*

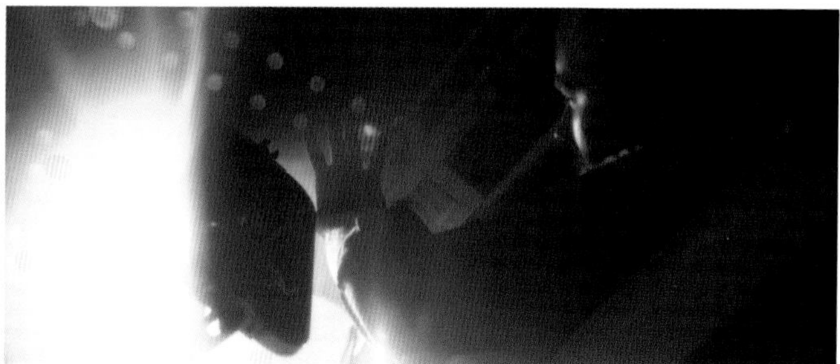

Roy's road adventure

shares with *Middletown* a recurrent conception of mainstream Middle America and its visible limitations under the pressures and promises of change: both works are about job precarity, about accumulative clutter in American homes consecrated to keeping up with the Joneses, about failure to mentor one's children, about marriage as a fraught process filled with misunderstanding (the Lynds' description of the Middletown housewife stuck at home could well apply to Ronnie Neary [Teri Garr] in *Close Encounters*: 'emotional ... Easily hurt, and largely incapable of facing facts or doing hard thinking'[2]). And both *Middletown* and *Close Encounters* narrate centrally how job precarity for a working-class man, along with internally fraught family precarity (the risk of domestic alienation), foster vulnerability to the *external* temptations of new life possibilities that derive, mysteriously yet temptingly, from beyond one's immediate surrounds. In 'Middletown', these glimpses of new potentialities might come from the movies or magazine ads or radio broadcasts, or they can derive, as in the case of *Close Encounters*, from the dazzling seductive spectacle of spiritual encounter out on the road.

If, by the end of *Close Encounters*, young Barry (Cary Guffey), after abduction by aliens, finds his way back to domesticity (as presumably does his mom, Jillian, who's pointedly told Roy she can't share his ultimate journey as she needs her son), Roy instead rejects family (the one he has with Ronnie and his kids, the one it's hinted he might create with Jillian and Barry). Barry re-finds the warmth of the maternal, but Roy turns away from domestic cares and caring to be enveloped in the aptly named '*mother*-ship'. The turn *to* fantastic escape is a turn *away from* worldly responsibility to follow instead some deeper imputed responsibility to one's own being. Along his journey, Roy not merely abandons children and spouse but seems for a while to step outside marriage through his bonding with Jillian, who has also had a 'close encounter'. Jillian initiates their connection by pretty much showing off her body (she pulls open her shirt to let him see her own UFO burn).[3] Later they share a deep, passionate kiss before he goes to the mother-ship, as if only a man can take this journey of discovery. An AFI poll by popular audiences may have found *Close Encounters* to be the 58th 'most inspiring' of American films, yet the movie firmly rejects some pretty entrenched American values around family, home and marriage. As one female viewer told me, 'If I were the wife, I would have bought him a one-way ticket on that UFO.' Or as another exclaimed, she would love a sequel devoted to all the therapy the abandoned Neary kids would need once their father left their lives![4]

If the Lynds worried about the effects of seductive modernity, the Seventies cinema of fascination literalises that seduction for (male) character and viewer alike. In leaving the house for the movie theatre (as we would have done in 1977 in order to see *Close Encounters*), we abandon domesticity, if only for a time, to let fantastic sights and sounds transport us to new universes of wondrous possibility. We would drive to the nearby multiplex, where often we would watch stories about characters who themselves also head off on the road but, generally in their case, *never to go back home*. Seventies cinema often seems to be about visual effect – the wow-inducing special effect in particular – but it is also often about escape, especially that of men who, alienated from their conventional lives, go off in search of something else.

Steps in a relationship

The ultimate trip (?)

Pointedly, if, as I contend, *Close Encounters* doesn't really need its viewers to believe in flying saucers, just overwhelming filmic spectacle, it also perhaps doesn't use its special effects for any higher end than dazzling viewers in the moment, via pure displays of cinematic visuality. The awe inspired by radiant, blinking lights, by the gadgets, gizmos and technologies of the aliens and scientists alike, doesn't likely turn into any kind of deep experience for the viewer. We get up from our seats, leave the light show and go home.

Certainly, in the moment of the 1970s, *Close Encounters* might have seemed trippy, and that's how the film's drug-addled co-producer Julia Phillips saw it: 'How am I to explain to D.B. [David Begelman, studio boss at Columbia] that anyone who has ever dropped acid and looked up at the sky for a while or smoked a joint ... is waiting for this movie.'[5] But more than Sixties head-trip films, *Close Encounters* targets a mainstream audience and works hard to remove any sense of a psychically induced experience, especially one that lasts past the movie's end. Yes, the glow of the flying saucers extends optically beyond the objects themselves, becoming a veritable abstract light show, especially through lens flaring that brilliantly suffuses the frame. Yet, under the credits, as the mother-ship makes its way into space, psychedelics give way to a narrative emphasis on Roy Neary's journey that eases the viewers out of the light-show spectacle that has gripped them over the last couple of hours and prepares them to return to their own anodyne existence.

Taking the ultimate trip in *2001: A Space Odyssey* (1968)

We might contrast the quest narrative here with the psychedelics of astronaut Dave Bowman's (Keir Dullea) Stargate journey, both cosmic and mental, in *2001: A Space Odyssey* (1968). That film, whose re-release poster pointedly told spectators to take 'the ultimate trip', certainly was enveloped in drug culture, and stories are legion of this or that spectator tripping out. In the Stargate sequence, for instance, cutaways to Dave's eyes, brightly re-coloured, suggest he is himself transforming both mentally and perhaps physically, beyond space, beyond time. *2001* renders this voyage of the human into an extraterrestrial realm overwhelmingly ambiguous: is, for instance, the star-child that Dave mutates into a force for good or for evil? In contrast, even if *Close Encounters* doesn't need us to believe in UFOs before or after we visit the movie theatre, it does want us to understand the UFO experience *in the movie's fictional story* as showing that one man learns what his close encounter with aliens means ultimately. There isn't mystery at the end but clarity.

In this respect, for all its dazzle, *Close Encounters* isn't just a cinematic abstraction of pure and moving visions and gripping sound. It tells a story, one that resolutely begins in the reality of an identifiable everyday world familiar to many of its viewers, even as it then chronicles how other-worldly possibilities plausibly enter in and alter everydayness decisively.

Earthly reality meets the other-worldly

As Bradley Schauer chronicles in *Escape Velocity: American Science Fiction Film, 1950–1982*, most science-fiction film in the immediate years after *2001* that aspired towards 'seriousness' did so by eschewing outer space and alien encounter (both of which *2001* has, in its own puzzle-making way) to look instead at futures *on Earth*, generally dystopian. As Schauer argues, *2001* was regarded inevitably as a one-off art-cinema venture into metaphysical ambiguities. (The 1984 sequel, *2010: The Year We Make Contact*, necessarily would explain away many such ambiguities.)[6]

Emphatically earthbound situations characterised science fiction in the first part of the 1970s. Admittedly, the tradition had started the same year as *2001* with the big hit *Planet of the Apes* (1968), followed by 1970s works that extrapolated from contemporary real-world politics, using the future to comment allegorically on dangerous trends in contemporary society.[7] In such films (titles include *Silent Running* [1972], *Soylent Green* [1973], *Death Race 2000* [1975], *Rollerball* [1975] and *Logan's Run* [1976], among others), a hero (usually white and male) initially serves dominant power until he sees the light (sometimes literally) and realises he is living inside a conspiracy he needs to break free from. Sometimes he makes it, sometimes he doesn't, and sometimes the outcome is unclear (will anyone at *Soylent Green*'s climax heed the protagonist's feverish warning that the soylent nutrient actually is

From the 'Special Edition': Roy inside the mother-ship

made from humans?). Such films, as we'll see, resemble the gritty everydayness of the so-called New Hollywood of the same moment in chronicling the breakdown of social life (often urban in locale), but they do so by extrapolation into a somewhere near future.

In contrast, while *Close Encounters* starts with dissatisfaction at earthly conditions, it soon seeks for answers *out in the stars*. It references 1950s science fiction in which aliens come to Earth, especially a minority tradition where their purpose is not invasion but the cause of galactic peace (*It Came from Outer Space* [1953], *The Day the Earth Stood Still* [1951]). In these earlier films aliens teach that humans' specific responsibility to the rest of the universe entails remaining *on Earth* to spread the word, while Roy Neary in *Close Encounters* departs Earth definitively, moving essentially away from worldly being to merge with extraterrestrial existence – and pretty much not doing anything to better the Earth he's leaving. Roy's transition from Earth to cosmos is also the film's transition from earthbound conventions of most science-fiction cinema just after *2001*.

Because of its big-budget effects-driven success, *Close Encounters* is often paired with *Star Wars* (also 1977), but the movies differ in many aspects. True, both centre on rebels against a dominant system, but *Star Wars*, in its us-versus-them outer-worldliness through to the shoot-'em-up battle at the end, stands as a generic science-fiction action-adventure movie, whereas *Close Encounters* converts any seeming adversarial nature of the aliens (for example, fleeting monster movie tropes in the attack on Jillian and Barry's farmhouse) into benign encounter.

Star Wars is a prime case of 'space opera', a derogatory term that intellectuals (including many serious-minded critics and science-fiction writers) employed across the history of the genre, both literary and cinematic, to describe pulpy directions that they feared targeted 'lowest common denominator' audiences through easy sensation rather than thoughtful reflection. Ironically, however, it was the space opera-ish *Star Wars*, and not the more existential, even spiritual, *Close Encounters* that received an Academy Award nomination for Best Picture (losing, though, to *Annie Hall* [1977]), a hint that high-octane effects-driven action cinema was transitioning from just-for-kids diversion to the mainstream of Hollywood cinema. An enumeration of the standard space opera elements of *Star Wars* pinpoints just how far *Close Encounters* differs. Space operas generally display: fast-moving spaceships among the stars; clear-cut conflict between humans and aliens (or helmeted de-humanised baddies in *Star Wars*), with robots also added to the mix; square-jawed action heroes (Han Solo or Luke Skywalker, who boldly introduces himself to Princess Leia, 'I'm Luke Skywalker; I'm here to rescue you'); but sometimes a campy irony towards the very idea of brawny heroics; romance, but of a chaste sort (Leia seems by film's end to be in a love triangle with Han and Luke); mystified and mystifying pseudo-science (jumps via hyper-drive, the 'Force' as the grounds for fantastic possibility); derring-do (swinging on ropes, wielding light sabres in close-quarter duels, zooming around meteors); and so on.

Star Wars and *Close Encounters* represent very different directions in science fiction, then. In this respect, it's useful again to cite Bradley Schauer on the genre as it moved through successive cycles, each imputing new modes of seriousness. In a manner that might well account for the success of *Close Encounters*, including with critics such as *The New Yorker*'s influential Pauline Kael, who ordinarily might well have objected to its emphasis on men-who-are-really-kids-deep-down, Spielberg's movie both helped initiate a new cycle of effects-driven films of diverting fantasy *and* offered a potent synthesis and exemplification of legitimating factors in all the previous cycles. To quote Schauer (with my thoughts on how this relates to *Close Encounters* in square brackets):

Depending on the historical period, different strategies have risen to prominence, including an emphasis on scientific accuracy [for example, press releases and production accounts that endlessly referenced *Close Encounters*' reliance on the UFO investigations of scientist J. Allen Hynek, especially his tripartite conceptualisation of 'close encounters'], the use of art cinema style and narration [for example, handheld camera or lens flares, which had come to signal New Hollywood cutting-edge style],[8] political content

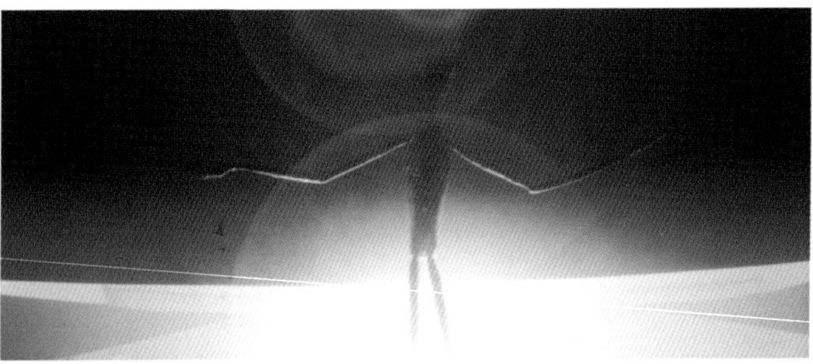

Lens flare as art-cinema style

[critique of government cover-up and of suburban banality], spectacular special effects [this goes without saying for *Close Encounters*!], greater psychological complexity and nuanced characterisation [Roy's alienation and search for a meaning in life, or Lacombe's position between authority and childlike love of aliens], the involvement of major stars [Richard Dreyfuss, associated with blockbusters like *American Graffiti* (1973) or *Jaws* (1975) and becoming a heartthrob in *The Goodbye Girl*, also from 1977], the guidance of an auteur director [Spielberg as increasingly an object of critical attention as crafted storyteller], the avoidance of camp [*Close Encounters* is not a frivolous work that doesn't take itself seriously], and fantasy world-building through production design [*Close Encounters* grounds its impact in the transition between two built ways of life – earthly worlds of suburbia and scientific investigation *and* the fantasy existence of aliens and UFOs].[9]

Whoosh

The narrative trajectory of *Close Encounters* works to get Roy, and the spectator, to accede, awestruck, to the uplift of a veritably psychedelic light show. I've asserted that *Close Encounters* is a film about *belief* – specifically, a belief in the aural and visual powers of cinema – but maybe 'belief' is too strong a word if it assumes *conscious* assent. Yes, Roy gains in knowledge along his quest – for example, television tells him that the mountain he's been fantasising about exists in reality and he learns where it is geographically – and, yes, *we* go along for the ride (literally a ride as Roy drives towards his

Voiceless amazement

destination and we accompany him). But the movie centrally enacts a surrender to sensory experience (soundtrack and visual effects) that is only partially an act of cognition, only partially articulated and idea-driven.

Here, we can reference film scholar Vivian Sobchack in her canonic study of science-fiction cinema, *The Limits of Infinity: The American Science Fiction Film, 1950–1975* (later expanded as *Screening Space: The American Science Fiction Film*).[10] To the extent, Sobchack argues, that the genre dramatises encounters with something fantastic yet possible (each work in the genre is both fiction *and* science), it is all about characters scrambling for discourses adequate to happenings beyond normal frameworks, maybe outside articulate cognition.

For example, as Sobchack chronicles, science fiction can depict attempts to evoke and invoke the fantastic through a language more lyrical or poetic: as she notes, 1950s science-fiction movies, for example, often sport florid discourse, especially in cheesily portentous voiceover narrations, as if grandiose speech could somehow match the grandeur of fantastic spectacle.

About the closest *Close Encounters* gets to poetic language, though, comes in the pathetic similes Ronnie employs to bring her husband's UFO experience back down to earthly reality: were the UFOs, she asks, shaped like 'a taco' or 'one of those Sara Lee moon-shaped cookies?'

Ronnie, 'largely incapable of facing facts or doing hard thinking'

Rather than a poetic language that might successfully invoke the heights of fantastic experience, *Close Encounters* frequently stages the breakdown of language. On the one hand, verbal account trails off into inarticulacy, as when Roy first tries to tell Ronnie what he experienced: 'I never would have believed it. There was this … Uh … In the cab there was this whole … It went … It was a … There was a red whoosh.' On the other hand, the film is replete with verbal repetition, as if people are stuck in frozen modes of expression that can't advance. Here are just some of the sentences that are repeated throughout the film: 'what's happening?'; 'this means something'; 'who are you guys?' And, of course, that Lacombe employs an English translator frequently entails direct repetition across languages (including the amusing moment when Laughlin [Bob Balaban] translates 'Pourquoi?' as 'Why?' and then Lacombe himself repeats 'Why?' in heavily accented fashion).

A striking example of one such verbal repetition occurs when Roy (with Jillian alongside) abruptly slams on the brakes as they are confronted by Devils Tower in actuality for the first time. To be accurate, *we* don't know initially what they're seeing: we merely see them looking with amazement off screen through the car window. Only after they leave the vehicle and climb a small embankment, as the music swells symphonically and the camera cranes up and then over them, is Devils Tower revealed *to us*. Twice, Jillian says 'I can't believe it's real,' to which Roy replies simply, 'It's real.' He then proposes they drive on to get closer to the towering mass. It's as if language can only go so far, and subsequently a deeper and extended immersion in the power and proof of ocular experience is required. (For what it's worth, Laughlin also thrice repeats 'I don't believe it' when the scientific team encounters a missing freighter that has turned up in the Gobi Desert.)

One fallback in science-fiction film when language is challenged to grasp the fantastic is a discourse of techno-rationality and scientific professionalism: it's how the emotionally empty astronauts speak in *2001*, as well as how scientists and engineers talk in *Close*

image that Spielberg himself declares he is most emotionally invested in across his illustrious career: the little boy Barry, viewed from behind, when he opens the front door to his home as it is besieged by aliens, an orange glow pouring over him from outside.[13] As Joseph McBride notes in his Spielberg biography, the director elaborates how that image can equally imply 'promise or danger outside that door' and thereby captures looking as an (open) act of assessment.[14] But even before positive or negative values are assigned to the image narratively (by characters, by the audience watching with them), the look beyond the frame stands first as a pure act of seeing. Or rather, as in the case of Barry looking past that open door, multiple ways of seeing: the shot of Barry succeeds one of his mother Jillian looking off screen in shock (as opposed to Barry's look of welcoming curiosity and wonder), and the cut then fills in what is frightening her – Barry at the door as unknown forces envelop him. And to the staggering of looks crafted by this editing, wherein we see a mother seeing and then cut to *what she is seeing*, we can add a third disposition of looking in the scene: out in the movie theatre we spectators are arrayed in front of the screen action as we see Jillian and then Barry as Jillian sees him. There is a relay of looks here but, importantly, they all stop at that radiant glow and don't go beyond it. Silhouetted by the open door of the farmhouse, Barry sees and we (and Jillian) see him, along with the orange glow emanating from the background, but not much more than that. There remains something beyond.

Cinematography by Vilmos Zsigmond

Here, a few words are in order about cinematographer Vilmos Zsigmond's Oscar-winning contribution to that rendition of seeing (although he could well merit extensive discussion at multiple points in this study). For *Close Encounters*, Zsigmond masters a visuality that works between dark murkiness (this is a film quite often set at night-time) and radiance, frequently in the form of luminous beams that pierce that murkiness (not merely night but fogginess or smokiness). Spielberg and Zsigmond together fix on light that emerges from the background to pour over characters who are thus veritably silhouetted by it. It is revealing that two major cinematographers recruited to shoot additional on-location footage for the film – William Fraker and Douglas Slocombe – were assigned to daytime sequences where light largely *fills* the frame (rather than peeking out from one part of it): Fraker shot the Sonora scene that opens the film where brightness and dust swellings work together, and Slocombe was the cinematographer for the daytime sequence in India.

Spielberg offered a succinct summation of Zsigmond's essential contribution around the time of the movie's release: 'One thing I told Vilmos was that it was important that we create action with light. Not movement, not running, not chasing, not shoot-outs, but light is the action of *Close Encounters*.'[15]

For a film whose very title hints at multiple possible modes of alien encounter, *Close Encounters* likewise offers multiple ways of

Looking at blips on a screen

seeing (and, as the scary noises of the farmhouse assault confirm, of hearing, as well). In the film's first scene (Sonora) and its second (Indianapolis flight control centre), we don't so much see UFOs as traces of their visitation: planes mysteriously appearing in the desert after decades; a man who recounts in Spanish (repeating his words) how the sun came out at night and sang to him; blips on a radar screen that air traffic controllers observe with a language of professionalism that sticks dryly to the rulebook (repetition: 'Do you want to report a UFO? Do you want to report a UFO?' 'I don't want to report one of those. I don't want to report one of those either').

Towards the end of the film, when Jillian and Roy have climbed to the far side of Devils Tower and discovered the scientists/engineers' staging site, Roy asks Jillian, 'Are you seeing what I'm seeing?' The corresponding reverse shot reveals the site as itself a special effect, a composite that combines live action, mattes, animation eventually (of the UFOs when they arrive), and so on.

The stage is set for the increasingly complex effects that show off alien encounter. That show is, quite simply, awesome. Yet I think it's significant that Jillian and Roy's first, earlier, sighting of Devils Tower in its physical reality – after it's been represented by mud, shaving cream, a pillow, drawings, a large-scale sculpture and a television broadcast – is presented as relatively unmediated live action: from their look off screen, to their movement out of

Shot/reverse shot

the car and up the embankment, the camera cranes up to record the impressive physical reality before Roy and Jillian *and* us. In that moment, the film is not about special effects – or maybe it's recognising that a weird piece of real geography has a specialness all its own.

An American sublime

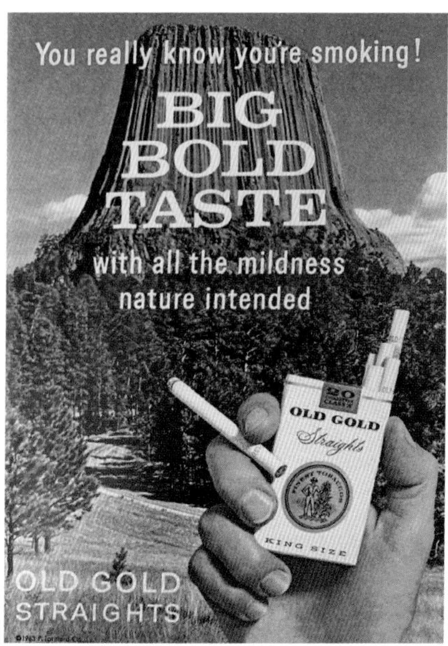
You really know you're smoking!
BIG
BOLD
TASTE
with all the mildness
nature intended
OLD GOLD
Straights
KING SIZE
OLD GOLD
STRAIGHTS
An American sublime (© P. Lorrilard Co., 1963)

Of course, the music and the soaring movement of the crane add emotion to the image but fundamentally that image is an indexical capturing of a reality that, no matter how awe-inspiring, is still within *our* possible and probable reality. Devils Tower, for what it's worth, was the very first US National Monument (declared as such in 1906). Some spectators of *Close Encounters* would have visited the site before 1977, and many more would do so after the film was released. In its appeal to nature, along with masculinised bigness and boldness, Devils Tower has a particular resonance in American popular culture.[16]

Ways of seeing

Close Encounters enables, then, a range of ways that the look at a foreboding or fascinating object registers in the mind of character and spectator *alike*. But also *unalike* in a way: having chosen to watch this movie, we know before Roy Neary that we're going to be seeing UFOs and that they'll probably be doing some pretty cool special-effects-driven stuff.

Early in the film, the improbable, almost blinding lights that shine down on Roy inspire in him obsessive curiosity: not dreading what he sees but not yet seduced by the escape from worldly cares they ultimately offer, for Roy the lights stand initially as marks of curiosity, something he is driven to figure out. And that he *drives* to figure out: as we'll return to, *Close Encounters* quickly becomes for a while a road movie before it ends up as a journey-into-outer-space movie.

In the middle of the film, a visit by the aliens to Jillian's isolated farmhouse is treated as more horrific than Roy's first encounter. It's now a veritable home invasion, with Jillian's son Barry pulled from his mother towards the unknown. Yet even here, there's the sense – common to a number of Spielberg films – that children might well have deeper fore*sight* than adults, are more trusting in cosmic wonders and can see the ultimate good in what first appears to the older generation as downright menacing. For instance, in that staggered relay of looks from mother to son at the door, we see horror on Jillian's face but trust on the part of Barry.

By film's end, the aliens release Barry back to his ecstatic mom – ecstatic both at her son's return and at her inspired viewing of the emanating glows of the UFO mother-ship that Barry emerges from. Roy, pretty much a child-man, trades places in a way with Barry, entering the mother-ship with innocently trusting awe. As one scholar, Dan North, writes in an essay on visual fascination across Spielberg's films, Roy 'is the ideal subject of spectacular perception, a man positioned to receive the rewards of the marvelous'.[17] (I might substitute 'has become' for 'is', as Roy has *to journey* to attain that reward – has, that is, to undergo a narrative series of visual experiences that end as redemptive, albeit initially ambiguous in tone, if not sometimes downright menacing [for example, at one point, lights in the sky that turn out not to be awe-inspiring UFOs but dread-inducing Army helicopters of a sort that menace UFO believers at several points in the film]).[18]

Ultimately, sight provokes what Vivian Sobchack describes, with regards to *Close Encounters*, as 'a new iconography of beatific human wonder, editorially linking affect to effect. Heads tilted, eyes gazing upward with childish openness and unfearful expectancy.'[19] The plural here is important. From visible traces of UFO visitations

(planes in the desert, blips on a screen, sunburn on an old man's face), to one man's lone encounter out on the road, to a shared experience of alien home invasion (even if Barry and Jillian each assess the visitation quite differently), *Close Encounters* portrays seeing throughout as humanly – and humanely – shared. Seeing, and experiencing, are an energetic communal activity engaged in by multiple characters and audience members alike.

To be sure, at the very end, Roy goes it alone, entering the mother-ship to blast off to his destiny. But along the way, he's taken into various communities: the surrogate family of Jillian and Barry, the collection of UFO believers that he joins on the hillside and at a press conference (and a second scene at the hillside includes pointed close-ups of characters we never see again, as if to acknowledge that Roy is only one among many, even if alone at

Cult community

the end), and the scientists that take him under their wing to prepare him for space flight.

In this respect, even though Spielberg would describe his aliens project early on as 'UFOs and Watergate', he and the film's producers, Julia and Michael Phillips, were insistent that one reason they turned from Paul Schrader's initial scripts – very much in the mode of the paranoid-conspiracy films that dotted the landscape of Seventies cinema, with shadowy state operations, intrepid heroes uncovering perfidy, suicides and maybe even murders – was precisely that the moment of cinematic conspiracy had been played out. (More about the Schrader scripts later.) Instead, *Close Encounters* moves beyond conspiracy by its end and, along the way, takes some inspiration from the more optimistic entries within the genre, in which the conspirators fail to keep knowledge under wraps. If Roy departs Earth with the aliens, Jillian takes photos of them, thereby ensuring that news of the discovery can be brought to the world at large. The hero is not the victim of a conspiracy, and there is every implication that others will learn of his accomplishment.

Far from spying on covert operations to end up perhaps as a victim of conspiracy, Roy joins with the team (the community of scientists, engineers and so on who have, in secrecy, planned the meeting with aliens at the mountain), even donning an official uniform to enter the mother-ship (that the aliens pick Roy out of the line doesn't contradict the fact that Lacombe and his scientific confreres had imagined him as only a single teammate within an expert group).

It's noteworthy that while the military appears initially as an obstacle to the believers' quest, from the menacing helicopters that break up the hillside community of UFOlogists to the strait-laced officers and soldiers who try to spirit Roy and Jillian and others away from Devils Tower, any such military presence fades away when Roy and Jillian make it to the scientists' staging site. There, everything is about the group working together and *applauding* their successes at alien encounter.

The sound of hands clapping

In fact, from around the mid-1970s, many Hollywood movies are filled with characters, often secondary ones, clapping when witnessing something marvellous, something that inspires rapturous outburst. Importantly, where viewers who saw *Close Encounters* in 1977 were wont to clap delightedly at spectacular imagery, characters *within the story* likewise seem impelled to react in similar fashion.

Obviously, people applauded in films before but often at planned celebratory events (Connie and Carlo's wedding in *The Godfather* [1972], for instance) or staged performances, where demonstrative approval was a logical response (for example, films set in a show business or theatrical world). But now, in the 1970s and after, it was often worldly, realistically rooted happenings that got witnesses celebrating. For example, by 1982 it could be newly graduated Officer and Gentleman Zack Mayo (Richard Gere), in his shiny white uniform, rescuing townie Paula Pokrifki (Debra Winger) from factory-floor drudgery while all the other workers leave their machines to clap boisterously (even jealous co-worker Lynette [Lisa Blount] gets with it and cheers – 'Way to go, Paula! Way to go!'). Or it could be 1986's *Crocodile Dundee*, where New Yorkers on a subway platform hoist Dundee (Paul Hogan) over their heads to reunite him with girlfriend Sue (Linda Kozlowski), to the applause of everyone in the station – a quite accurate portrayal of the typical New Yorker bystander. (I'm being sarcastic.)

Applauding a close encounter

In *Close Encounters*, there are multiple scenes of characters celebrating boisterously the unexpected mysteries of the universe. Significantly, applause doesn't necessarily seem the most appropriate response in many such moments. Near the end of the film, for instance, when UFOs come dancing from the skies with pulsating lights and pick up on the musical tones beaming towards them, the corresponding reaction of the earthlings is to engage in rapturous applause. Maybe this culminating outburst of approval is to some extent narratively plausible, but it still seems somewhat improbable for these geeky engineers to give in to such frenetic behaviour. But the applause works to create a pathway from these professionals within the film to the audience members outside it. Maybe we don't applaud at the very same moment, but we are impelled to enact our delight throughout the film – whoops, enraptured laughter (the audible chuckle of the audience when, already having signalled a car to go around his truck, Roy does the same as a second set of lights appears from behind and then rises upward as it's actually a UFO).

Here, it is noteworthy that one moment of applause in *Close Encounters* comes not in response to visuals but to sound: the playback at a meeting of scientists, engineers, government officials and astronauts of the recording of men in India chanting the five-tone melody that came from the skies. The prior sequence had ended with a spectacular sight: asked to identify the origin of those notes, the multitude suddenly points, each and every man, upward

Community

with vigour. This is followed by a sharp cut to the packed auditorium, where the recording is being played to the assemblage. It's not just images that inspire in *Close Encounters* but sounds too, and that goes both for characters in the movie *and* viewers, who become part of a community on screen and off.

Cocoons of sound

Close Encounters owes so much of its impact to its *soundtrack*, especially if we take that to mean more than just background music. Of course, John Williams's score has much to do with the aural power of the film, running from rousing symphony, to quieter background, to a sort of experimentalism *within* the narrative through the aliens' five-tone signal – intentionally not the three tones that would constitute simple melody but something a bit more complex, hinting at melodic closure but deliberately not fulfilling it.[20]

Beyond its music, *Close Encounters* involves a very consequential mix of aural elements (literally a mix, since many scenes overlay sounds, such as pounding wind over dialogue struggling to be heard in the opening desert scene). Sound editor Frank Warner notes how some sounds could be big and loud – for example, the differing but dynamic qualities of that desert wind in each shot – but he also celebrates the power of silence. As he puts it,

Steven Spielberg and John Williams

> When an accustomed sound stopped, it became a signal that something big was about to happen. Then, when the shattering experience was all over and everything had become visually peaceful again, we'd start the sound up very subtly. Maybe just one cricket at first, then two, then a distant dog barking.[21]

Importantly, the movie's production and release overlapped with, and benefited from, the roll-out of Dolby Stereo, which in the 1970s became the preferred format for movie theatre sound. Theatres that hadn't actually converted to stereo might still exploit Dolby branding, not an entirely inaccurate stratagem, since many were already using Dolby's prior noise-reduction system. Dolby *Stereo*, on the other hand, attractively combined three front channels of sound (Left, Right, Centre behind the movie screen, with dialogue sent expressly to the centre) with a surround channel of speakers dispersed throughout the space of the auditorium (side and back walls).

Dolby Stereo had been used sporadically for rock documentaries and music-heavy features (most notably, 1976's pop musical *A Star is Born*). The success of *Star Wars*, strong in sound design, fostered an association of Dolby with science fiction and encouraged more and more theatres to convert to stereo/surround sound. In an interview around the time of *Close Encounters*' release, Spielberg even touted his own movie's potential impact on expansive conversion to stereo:

> Hopefully with every movie I make I'll be able to contribute between 50 and 75 new Dolby sales for that film. So in two years perhaps there will be a thousand theaters in this country that can show a movie with its full dynamic range.[22]

Dolby essentially offered two stereo systems: Dolby Stereo 70mm six-track magnetic sound (perfect for big movie palaces) and Dolby Stereo 35mm optical-track. The initial roadshows for *Close Encounters* at New York's Ziegfeld Theatre and Los Angeles's Cinerama Dome were in 70mm, and a few other metropolitan palaces employed that format as the film went on wider release. Exhibition, then, was a blend of 70mm Dolby, Dolby 35mm and mono 35mm.[23]

While the variety of formats meant that not everyone would hear the movie in stereo, *Close Encounters* was recorded and mixed with stereo possibilities in mind. Again, sound editor Frank Warner describes the challenges as well as the possibilities: 'For the stereo prints we were able to run them all over the screen. We were recording "true" stereo, in which you actually move the sound and dialogue.' (When, at the UFO-debunking press conference, a news crew pans to the old codger [Roberts Blossom] who pipes up that he once saw Big Foot, we can take this as an in-joke about the physical shift to new sources of dialogue that stereo could invoke.) And Warner cites the long encounter with the aliens at the film's ending as a particularly complex sound exercise:

There's an awful lot of communication going on in those scenes, plus the sounds of computer equipment, movie cameras, still cameras and video rigs. Added to this was the reverberation caused by the surrounding hills. All in all, there was more of this type of what we call 'full-layer' sound than I've ever encountered in a single feature before.[24]

Sound scholar Bill Whittington sums up the surround sound design this way:

The ultimate example of this playfulness [with enveloping sound] is represented in the final sequence of *Close Encounters of the Third Kind*, in which the surround channels carry the sounds of the alien crafts jetting by, the reverberate radio chatter from the government controllers, and the mutual tones of communication and music. The scene places audience and characters alike into a visual and sonic playpen of fantasy and science fiction.[25]

Not merely was the sound of *Close Encounters* often *loud* (often *VERY* loud), from symphonic blares to moments engineered by Warner in which an original sound might be replaced by something more dynamic (for example, a complicated nail and string system for the scene of the screws coming undone at Jillian's farmhouse – 'It was going big that got the sound, not trying to do a little tiny screw sound,' as Warner puts it). It also mattered that a dominant sound was *low rumbles* (UFOs landing, UFOs passing overhead). As top Dolby scholar Gianluca Sergi reiterated by email as he walked me through Dolby Stereo of the 1970s:

Very low frequencies were used to attempt reaching out at an audience physically, not merely figuratively, providing a level of engagement that we now call immersive but at the time was new and thrilling. ... low frequencies could be reproduced by cinema speakers in ways that were simply not possible before. ... In short, deeper bass sounds, omnidirectional/filling up a theatre had become available to anyone mixing in Dolby Stereo and any theatre willing to install their system.[26]

As Sergi adds, low-frequency sounds, like the recurrent rumbles in *Close Encounters*, tend to feel omnidirectional so that even monaural projection of the film would somewhat evoke a surround soundscape (aided, perhaps, by a sort of 'placebo effect' wherein Dolby branding, whatever this actually meant, might make spectators believe they were hearing surround sound).

As a striking example of the film's effective utilisation of multiple sound channels, between front speakers and surround, Sergi cites

> John Williams's one-note crescendo that becomes progressively louder until it literally explodes with a bang and a cut to the bright desert scene [after the blackness of the credits] that opens the movie. That 'bang' warns audiences that the film is going to be a visceral experience from the get-go, just as *Star Wars*'s overhead flying ships in its opening sequence had alerted the audience to the arrival of contemporary surround sound to the cinema. It felt as though you were completely enveloped, no place to hide. ... Once all senses were straining to make sense of the widening sound field, the sonic boom/bang would deliver the *coup de grâce*, followed immediately by an assault on the audience's sense of vision.[27]

That dynamic opening, it is worth noting, is also *visually* an exercise in the powers of cinema: from darkness to blinding light, to the two car headlights that emerge bit by bit from the obscurity of the sandstorm, to signal the first narrative actions of the movie.

A movie begins: let there be light!

The cinema of 1977

By 1977, 'Steven Spielberg' was on its way to being the name of a cultural brand as much as a person. Spielberg mattered (and still matters) because the world at large had made him matter in the popular discourse of movie culture. That discourse, including the mass journalism of renowned film critics, frequently imagined him as a particularly gifted storyteller, either (depending on which critic) a consummate entertainer whose diverting movies generally hit the mark for craft perfection or a would-be thinker who was using the guise of entertainment to make some salient comments about the things we fear or embrace, and the values of life we yearn for. An auteur, that is.

Moreover, this moment in the 1970s marked a point when production expenses and star salaries, and especially box office, all began to be widely reported on in that same popular press in a manner unprecedented. The *business* of entertainment became fodder for public discussion and came itself to play a role in marketing,

Steven Spielberg with *Close Encounters* editor Michael Kahn

insofar as achieving blockbuster status (as most Spielberg films did) made it imperative to see the movies everyone else was seeing. To Spielberg as entertainer and 'thinker' was added the identity of astute businessman.[28]

One early argument was that somehow Spielberg had tapped into the American zeitgeist, intuiting what audiences appeared to want from popular entertainment. There were both positive and negative versions of this argument: Spielberg's movies, like some others of that moment, were said to offer cheerful optimism and triumph, so needed after the wound to the American (masculine) psyche from defeat in Vietnam; *or*, it was said that that very optimism was a path to blinkered self-denial as America turned from self-critique to easy feel-goodness.

Whatever the case, it is unlikely that any one movie sums up the times – that it captures a spirit of the moment, as if there were only one valence to a historical period. Pointedly, perhaps predictably, not every film at the time focused on the upbeat or did so specifically by narrating a man's spiritual quest to find life's meaning. In fact, that was a very rare occurrence in the films of the period. Having watched more than three-quarters of the 140 or so Hollywood releases of 1977, I can attest that none, other than Spielberg's film, veritably involve spiritual quest, even generously defined. Even the rare science-fiction film (a genre, as noted earlier, with in fact very few fantasy offerings through the first part of the 1970s until *Close Encounters* or *Star Wars*) would often substitute an earthbound journey for fantasy out in space: in the case of *Damnation Alley*, for instance, there's a quest but it's worldly, not spiritual, as a group of survivors of nuclear apocalypse take to the road and find a cheerful, welcoming rural community at film's end.

Revealingly, most films of 1977 that involve alien encounters belong more to horror cinema than to science fiction or fantasy (though, of course, these genres can overlap), and it is worth noting that the famous set-piece in *Close Encounters* of the extraterrestrials' visit to Jillian and Barry's isolated farmhouse plays like a horror

Home invasion?

movie assault (some writers compare it to the avian attack on domesticity in Hitchcock's *The Birds* [1963]). It's all about unseen beings intruding into the sanctity of private space and doing so with violent effect (electric gadgets come to life, floor screws mysteriously come undone, and so on). No doubt, the end of the film – when Barry is reunited with his mother; where we and the movie's humans finally get to meet the aliens; where we and the humans realise they ultimately mean no harm and, quite the contrary, are there to foster alien–earthling interaction – makes up for the horror. Yet the experience of the homestead assault sequence is undeniably quite unnerving – for both Jillian and us as spectators, who witness the trauma of a child wrenched, seemingly irrevocably, from his mother's arms to disappear within a UFO into the skies.

Like *Close Encounters*, some horror films of the moment try to provide a real-life explanation for what might initially seem to be happenings, close to supernatural, that push at the limits of our reality (*Close Encounters* relies, after all, on the premise that it is possible, and perhaps even plausible, that aliens might engage with our earthly ways of life). However believably or not, such horror films, to stay with 1977 alone, try to find possible scientific explanations for monsters, whether mutation from radiation (*The Hills Have Eyes* or *Damnation Alley* or *The Empire of the Ants*), or laboratory invention (*Demon Seed*'s monster computer), abandoned dogs gone rabid

(*The Pack*), and even beasts of the wild crazed by rays of the sun after ozone layer depletion (*Day of the Animals*), and so on. Yet, other films move the encounter with aliens into much more of a fantasy realm (it's worth remembering that the humans of *Star Wars* are actually *not* earthlings, since opening titles clarify that they're from 'A long time ago in a galaxy far, far away ...'). And, no doubt influenced by the enormous horror blockbuster earlier in the decade, *The Exorcist* (1973), a number of 1977 horror films suggest a supernatural (and not really natural) origin to monsters – from, for instance, satanic realms (the title of the exploitation film *Satan's Cheerleaders* makes the devilish connections explicit). Whereas *Close Encounters* offers a scientific rationale as to how (and why) aliens come to visit, the satanic films simply imagine a supernatural evil out there that gets unleashed for little reason: it is never explained, for instance, how and why the demonic vehicle of *The Car* came to be possessed by the Devil. (For what it's worth, *The Car* seems doubly inspired by Spielberg's monstrous-attack films: the music that accompanies the car's recurrent attacks seems to be channelling *Jaws*, while the very premise of relentless onslaught by a vehicle with no visible driver harks back to Spielberg's TV horror tale *Duel* from 1971).

Actually, the most quantitatively dominant movie trend of 1977 is, like *Close Encounters*, very much about getting out on the road *but to a very different end* (or, pun intended, very different *ending*). This is the cinema of the good-ole country boy, usually Southern, who drives around his hometown area in a fast car or a big rig (or sometimes a motorcycle), boozin', brawlin', hell-raisin', womanisin', trying all the while to keep at bay the smokeys (portly, often racist, cops in their black-and-white vehicles). *Smokey and the Bandit* is the best known – and most successful – of the good-ole boy films, which often didn't enjoy distribution outside the South or Midwest, where they were screened especially in drive-in circuits; but the movies were numerous, feeding no doubt into contemporary sociological currents around working-class men and whiteness, and a romanticisation of life on the road. Even Henry Fonda got in on the act with *The Great*

Smokey and the Bandit (1977)

Smokey Roadblock. Interestingly, a movie from this cycle almost served as Spielberg's feature debut, as he worked on development for a good-ole boy film with Burt Reynolds, ultimately released as *White Lightning* in 1973, with Joseph Sargent filling in as director.

Unlike the alienated road movies of the first part of the 1970s (about which more later), but also unlike *Close Encounters*, good-ole boy movies show their contented, easy-going protagonists happy with their chosen lifestyle and determined, indeed, to do whatever it takes to keep it going. In some cases, they head to new places (the Henry Fonda character in *The Great Smokey Roadblock*, dying of cancer, wants one last successful cargo run to Florida), but most often taking to the road entails a cyclicity as the good-ole boy makes a score (for example, doing the rounds with moonshine) and returns to base to start all over again. It is clearly less the goal of taking to the road that matters than all the fun along the way: in *Smokey and the Bandit*, Bandit (Burt Reynolds) is delegated a pretty silly 'mission' – crossing state lines to bring Coors beer back to a patron – and what matters most are the fisticuffs and fast pursuits and smokey pile-ups en route. To be sure, one thing that changes for these guys on the road is that they sometimes meet up with a woman who turns out to be special, and she ends up coming along for the ride (unlike *Close Encounters*, where Roy leaves all women behind as he blasts off into outer space).

As I've argued for *Close Encounters*, these films also *believe in cinema*: they offer a site (and sight) of spectacular visual effects (crashes, for instance) that often push plot credibility and even narrative itself to the side: for example, the 1977 motorcycle movie *Sidewinder 1* starts with more than five minutes of racing footage that only minimally gets any story going. The films believe in action for its own sake as its own purpose and disperse plot into set-pieces of dynamic crashes (but in loving slo-mo). In contrast to *Close Encounters*, then, where Roy finds an answer to his nervous quest for meaning in the massively effects-driven spectacle on Devils Tower, across their running length the good-ole boy films offer endless spectacular physical effects (not photographically composited ones), such as interminable chases and pile-ups as vehicles and cargo shatter across the screen, implying an ongoing sense of action that is fun in itself but without narrative purpose. (Given the timing of production, it is likely a coincidence, albeit uncanny, that in *The Great Smokey Roadblock* the protagonist encounters a stoner, played by Austin Pendleton, whose first words are all about an extraterrestrial close encounter, in which his car lost power and he was bathed in an intense eerie light from above.)

Seventies 'New' and 'Newer' Hollywood

[F]rom 1970 to at least 1977, every other movie that came out *did* seem like it was about '*some guy and his problems*'.

Quentin Tarantino[29]

Close Encounters arrives only just in time to save us from the dust-collectors, the grave-yard souls, the self-destroyers, the Doom Makers who, whether they speak with the sick manic scream of a Martin Scorsese or the epileptic soprano of Ken Russell, invite us to slit our wrists, hang up our skins, and give over to the Death Wish.

Ray Bradbury on feel-good religiosity in *Close Encounters*[30]

Within its narrative world and within the cultural and political space of the decade, *Close Encounters*, as a 1977 blockbuster, stands as a film of *transition* – of Roy's transition to a new way of being, of *Hollywood*'s transition to blockbuster films of redemption and transcendence and all-round feel-goodness.

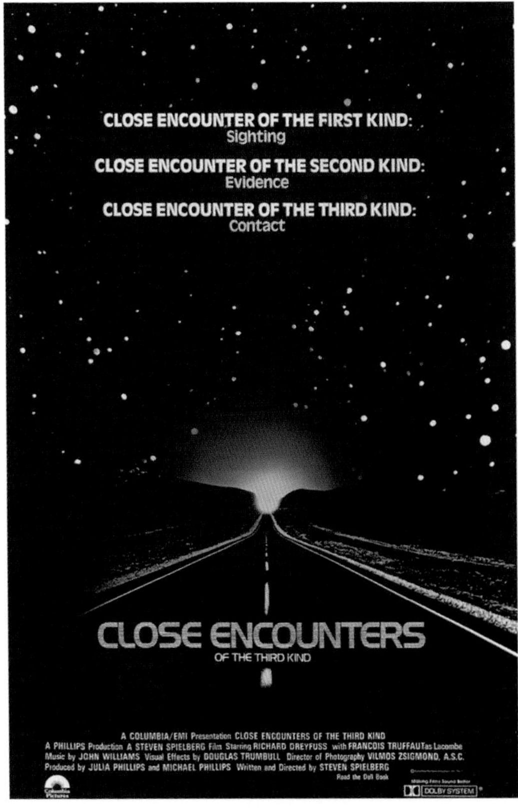

In key ways, Roy is not unlike many figures (mostly men) of earlier Seventies *road movies* who feel called away from domesticity towards an open-ended destiny. Indeed, the iconic ad for *Close Encounters* shows an open highway leading towards a mysterious glowing horizon, making the connection to the Seventies road movie fairly explicit.

Just as Bobby Dupea's existential quest in *Five Easy Pieces* (1970) means leaving girlfriend Rayette stranded along the road, far from home, so too there's a male-privileged immorality to Roy's actions. (When I screened the film with some neighbourhood kids, aged 9–11, they said what most bothered them was Roy abandoning his family. I'd pre-warned them that the siege of Jillian and Barry's farmhouse might scare them – and they did find one close-up of floor vent screws coming undone somewhat unsettling – but what really frightened them was witnessing a family coming undone as the dad turns his back on domesticity.)

It is a common gesture by film historians to posit a break between an initial Seventies questioning cinema of gritty and downbeat realism (think *Taxi Driver* [1976] with its broken-

down city, fatuous politicians and endemic violence) *and* a later cinema of upbeat escapism literalised in special effects fantasies of transcendence. Revealingly, each period has been claimed, mutually exclusively in some cases, to represent a 'New Hollywood'.

Yet it is easy to overstate the distinction. Many films across the period combine realistic everyday entrapment with dreams of escape. To take just one example of how realist and fantasy modes of cinema blur in the period, *Saturday Night Fever*, released in the same year as *Close Encounters*, sets the bulk of its narrative in mean-streets Brooklyn, presented from the first shot as a site of working-class burden, if not downright entrapment (Tony's bounce weighted down by the paint can he carries for work). Tony (John Travolta) and his gang can get some buoyant respite at the science-fictional discotheque aptly named 2001: Space Oddyssey (*sic*), where gleaming lights promise possibilities no less seductive than the luminous glow of the UFOs in *Close Encounters*. (At the time, some critics made the connection direct by referring to the colours in the Spielberg film as 'disco ball'.) But 'escape' in *Saturday Night Fever* seems somewhat contained and constrained (just one disco venue within the confines

Taking the ultimate trip in 2001: Space Oddyssey in *Saturday Night Fever* (1977)

of Brooklyn), and evanescent: as the advertising tagline for the film put it, 'Where do you go when the record's over?' Like *Close Encounters* to a degree, *Saturday Night Fever* links back to the earlier films of a New Hollywood about male alienation, while it shares with the science-fiction movie some strong degree of fantasy: Travolta's dance moves almost defy gravity in a way that seems to grant him magical powers; Manhattan, across the river but a universe apart, is a fantasy reconstruction of everyday reality where you can always find a free parking space and where would-be rapists can find redemption from their would-be victims.

Importantly, if the purposeless anti-hero that pervades the New Hollywood of the first part of the 1970s is a transition from an older Hollywood, Roy Neary is in key ways a transition *from* that sort of character to someone more determined, more resolute, more – in a word – purposeful. While, in the initial phases of the movie, Roy is not sure what message he should garner from his close encounter ('This means something,' he asserts to Ronnie as he stares at the mound of shaving cream in his hand), he knows assuredly that there *is a message* and needs to find out what it is and what its implications are for him. To make a weak pun, if the anti-heroes of the New Hollywood are often shown driving – even if their 'action' is a meandering one that gets them nowhere – Roy exhibits *drive* to get *somewhere*.

Out on the road, Roy, like so many (white) men across America's cultural history, finds open space a possible path to empowerment. For instance, when he explains to Jillian that the only way to get past the military roadblocks is off-road, she assents and he goes crashing through fences in a mad dash across countryside. Indeed, we can note how *Close Encounters* often plays on tensions of open spaces that Roy moves through in his expansive quest (including open *outer* space at the film's non-ending ending) *and* interior spaces that he is closed up in, confined in, starting with the crammed interior of his home. Conversely, although Jillian accompanies Roy on his road trip, she is much more associated with lack or failure of motion – running ineffectually after Barry outside their farmhouse (she does

Jillian watches approvingly as Roy heads out into the cosmos

this twice) and shown quite often virtually flattened against some static background (an elevator's interior space, a motel room wall, the inside panel of a military van, even the imposing rocks at Devils Tower). Jillian stays behind, of course, while Roy accedes and ascends to new life possibilities.

In the moment of transition from New Hollywood to the newer feel-good variety, *Saturday Night Fever* could end in freeze-frame as Stephanie (Karen Lynn Gorney) and Tony lean in towards each other in her Manhattan apartment: like Roy, Tony was moving towards a realm of new possibility (including, in this case, Stephanie's forgiveness for his earlier attempt to rape her), and the freeze keeps that open. For its own ending, *Close Encounters* prefers lyrical shots of the mother-ship transporting Roy to destinations unknown over the open-endedness of the freeze-frame, but it too imagines redemption ahead for the male figure.

Perhaps no portrayal of an outer-space destination could ever have brought sufficient closure to Roy's journey. Perhaps the fact that he has found inner peace – exhibited in the radiance of his benighted look – means that we don't need any further imaging of other-worldliness.[31]

In fact, any closure to Roy's story comes as much from secondary elements as much as from explicit narrative finality: the uplift of John Williams's symphonic score, the beneficence of the alien creatures, Lacombe's wistfulness in seeing Roy off on his journey and his hopeful hand signals to one of the alien creatures, and so on. In a way, none of these elements actually *proves* that what is to happen *next* to Roy will be definitely and definitively good. Indeed, with its notorious ability to proffer subversive readings of big Hollywood films, *Mad* magazine ends its *Close Encounters* parody, *Clod Encounters of the Absurd Kind* from July 1978, with a pointedly downbeat imagining of what happens next: readying himself to enter the mother-ship, 'Cloy' buoyantly and sanctimoniously tells a sceptical 'Jelly' that 'People believe in other worlds because they **know** there's something better somewhere, some **higher form of civilization**, where the human spirit can soar, **free** and **untrammeled**, and where **life** has **real meaning!** That's what I expect to find aboard **this ship!**', only to discover with dismay (in the last panel) that all the aliens do on board is bicker ('All you know how to do is **spend, spend, spend**'; 'You **drink** so much you **can't see straight**' [reply: 'If I could **see straight**, I'd have to look at YOU!!']).

The flip side to *Close Encounters*' benign but open-ended invitation and initiation into alien lifestyle also transpires in a famous episode of *The Twilight Zone*, 'To Serve Man' (CBS, 1962), where the earthly protagonist, about to enter the alien spaceship, pretty much like Roy ascending the ramp into the mother-ship, is warned by his assistant, rushing up, that what earthlings thought was a code book about inter-world cooperation is actually the aliens' *cookbook* for turning humans into outer-space sustenance. The warning comes too late and the spaceship's ramp shuts up tight, entrapping the protagonist. (Later on, a revered recurrent sketch on *Saturday Night Live* [NBC, 1975–] dealt with a Ms Rafferty [Kate McKinnon], who, it must be admitted, fit a certain stereotype of white working-class 'trailer trash' and recounted in ever more colourful language how her alien encounters had involved increasingly outrageous sexual improprieties on the part of the extraterrestrials. In her farewell appearance on the show, McKinnon as Ms Rafferty headed up the UFO ramp in a light-bathed goodbye, having learned that the aliens wanted a human to accompany them back to their planet and she, only somewhat begrudgingly, volunteered herself for the mission.)

What does it mean for *Close Encounters* to have both an open ending (Roy in transit in outer space) and a happy ending – Roy at peace with the universe, with John Williams's score, the approving looks of Jillian and Lacombe, the glow of lights and the radiance on his face all confirming he's found his way?

On the one hand, it matters perhaps that for the re-release of the film, the studio pushed Spielberg to add footage of Roy *inside* the mother-ship, as if there needed to be more glimpses of 'what comes next'. On the other hand, it's significant that the added footage still didn't bring closure: the spaceship remains on a journey to parts unknown.

Affirmative endings were not that common in the downbeat New Hollywood films of the first part of the decade. For instance, *Five Easy Pieces* merely trails off as Bobby exits the frame and leaves Rayette behind, with the strong implication of something veritably suicidal to his coatless departure into the biting cold of northern climes. In fact, as much as the anti-heroes in some New Hollywood films simply go off at the end, other narratives are downright fatalistic. At worst, death lies ahead out on the road (*Easy Rider* [1969]). Or if not death, defeat and a descent into passivity, including through

The non-ending ending of *Five Easy Pieces* (1970)

lobotomy inflicted by the forces that be (for example, *One Flew Over the Cuckoo's Nest* [1975]). In other cases, the anti-hero is pulled back into the world he tried, however briefly or furtively, to escape: rebels resume their regular careers in a defeat rendered as a sort of death-in-life (for instance, Jack Nicholson again, in *The Last Detail* [1973], who completes an onerous naval mission that he tried to resist).

Certainly, the buoyant, if open, ending of *Close Encounters* might seem appropriate to an America that was itself transitioning to conservative uplift under Reagan. Indeed, there was a tendency in 1980s film criticism to categorise *Close Encounters*, along with other rousing blockbusters from the late 1970s into the 1980s, as 'Reaganite entertainment', a celebration of assuredness after the malaise of the previous period. (Infamously, Jimmy Carter's 1979 television address about the challenges of austerity, crises of family bond and faltering faith in government quickly became known as the 'malaise speech', and his own declarations of acceptance of bleak conditions became a spur, under Reaganism, to go beyond those conditions).[32]

Yet, like the ill-fated anti-heroes of the earlier New Hollywood, Roy rejects those key American values that the Reaganite moment would hold dear: the movie offers no celebration of either family or commodity culture and the idea that personal possessions, such as leisure items, are a path to perfection. Roy initially hits the road in a rejection of suburban domesticity (which in turn rejects him as Ronnie drives away with the family, the neighbours looking impassively on, but, unlike Roy, heading in her case to an announced destination at the end of her 'road trip' – she's taking the kids to her sister's – so it's not an open-ended road movie for her).

It is a small detail yet noteworthy that, although he's sort of in a 'road movie', Roy is not really in possession or ownership of earthbound vehicles: he is driving a company truck when he has his initial close encounter; his spouse drives off in the Middle American family station wagon that we only once see him driving (with Ronnie beside him as he returns to the bend in the road that was the site of the UFO encounters but where, now, Ronnie sadly tries to get him to

'Where are we going?' 'Just get in the car!'

'snuggle' as they once did at such spots, only for Roy to look past her up at the sky); and he gets to Devils Tower by way of a rental car that is left behind when he and Jillian are rounded up by the military. It is equally worthy of note that Roy doesn't seem to do that well with any of these vehicles: he gets lost in both his company's truck and the rental car and, in virtually identical shots, has to spread a map in front of him, while during Ronnie's departure from their home he is violently knocked over by the station wagon as she desperately pulls away.

For what it's worth, it is rare to find movies from the period that centre on women out on the road in search of fulfilment (which is one reason why *Thelma & Louise* had such resonance when it came out in 1991: there seemed to have been little like it before). For all its apparent social critique, the so-called New Hollywood of the 1970s was actually quite antiquated in its stereotypes of pioneering men just itching to go off on adventure and its concomitant castigation of women who can't empathise with their quest. In road movies, home-bound women often stand for suffocating domesticity (Ronnie in *Close Encounters*, the pathetic Rayette in *Five Easy Pieces* [Karen Black received an Oscar nomination for Best Supporting Actress], the naïve Jerri Jo [Lee Purcell] in *Adam at Six A.M.* [1970]). Often, the few women who get on the road either rediscover entrapments similar to the stranglehold domesticity they tried to leave behind (the heroines in *Alice Doesn't Live Here Anymore* [1974] and *Wanda* [1970] encounter men who are as abusive as their husbands back home) or they can't seem to find anything like the fulfilment Roy Neary experiences. For instance, after the death of her abusive would-be bank-robber boyfriend, we last see Wanda (Barbara Loden) drinking in a bar with strangers, a freeze-frame leaving things ambiguous, certainly a non-ending nowhere as upbeat as Roy Neary's. More optimistically, Laurie (Didi Conn) in *You Light Up My Life* (1977) takes to the road from LA to New York to build her musical career in the Big Apple, but only *at the very end of the film* where a few shots of her driving give way to a montage of her soaring *Billboard* ranking to symbolise her willed move to a new life.

Spielberg's own earlier road movie, *The Sugarland Express* (1974), merits mention in this respect as it centres on a heterosexual *couple* on the road and gives equal attention to the woman's drive as much as the man's: here, a young woman gets her husband out of jail and goes on the road with him, but with the intention of reuniting with their child (so there is a goal to this road adventure, a very familial one). In the event, the husband dies and it's only an end title that tells us the woman eventually got her child back after doing jail time. Death mitigates any sense of a happy ending, unlike in *Close Encounters* where Jillian, like *Sugarland*'s Lou Jean (Goldie Hawn), is reunited with her child, *but* where Roy goes on to a heavenly, better place, not the grim death that catches up with *Sugarland*'s Clovis (William Atherton).

One of the few films of 1977 to feature a woman on the road at length is *Bobby Deerfield*, but it's not even an exception that proves the rule: the title character is a *male* racing car driver (Al Pacino) who takes as a road companion an escaped sanatorium patient Lillian Morelli (Marthe Keller) only, in an echo of 1970's *Love Story*, to have her die of her illness once he's fallen in love with her. In the road movie, journeying really is the province of men (like Lillian Morelli, Jillian in *Close Encounters* is passenger, not active protagonist).

Making a New Hollywood movie

Key to siting *Close Encounters* in the context of Seventies New Hollywood is the revealing fact that the first draft scripts were penned by Paul Schrader, soon after winning acclaim for his screenplay for that key work of early Seventies New Hollywood, *Taxi Driver*. (In fact, *Taxi Driver* and *Close Encounters* shared the same producers, Michael and Julia Phillips.) Few screenwriters took the alienated anti-hero to its New Hollywood extreme as Schrader. His scripts (and then the films he directed, like *American Gigolo* [1980]) centre obsessively on men trying to live by their own masculine code but finding that conventions and social pressures threaten to derail their existential personal project.[33]

Most of those who worked on the release version of *Close Encounters* suggest that Schrader's scripts differed significantly from what Spielberg was starting to want for his movie, and Schrader himself seems in interviews to indicate that his efforts were either ignored or abandoned. Yet, as we'll see, there's more of Schrader in the final film than legend has implied. I want to tell that story, but first it is useful to explain how the project initially came about and

Paul Schrader

evolved, both when Schrader came on board and then when and why he was subsequently removed from the project.

Much of the story of the film's production has been told before, most usefully by Ray Morton in his 2007 'Making of' volume, as well as Michael Klastorin's 'ultimate visual history', along with actor Bob Balaban's published daily diary on the film's production. The existing histories provide all the production anecdotes one might desire (including ideas that didn't work, such as suspending the extraterrestrials by wires to make them look as if floating).[34]

Importantly, much of the 'historiography' for *Close Encounters* is coincident with the movie's production and release. That is, from the outset, *Close Encounters* was accompanied by an industry-encouraged discourse that chronicled the film at close range and became itself part of the phenomenon, often serving as marketing. To take a key example, Bob Balaban's diary extends from his initial involvement through to the film's promotion and release and stands as a heartfelt memento account of the movie, filled with great stories.

Most rigorous as contemporary accounts are two special issues of journals concerned generally with *technical aspects* of movies in their pre-production, production and post-production phases. *American Cinematographer*, the official journal of the American Society of Cinematographers (but reaching beyond the professionals to amateur movie-makers and fans), examined, in a special January 1978 issue, the fabrication of *Close Encounters* by its vast creative team, with interviews from producer and director to cinematographer, set designer and special effects co-ordinator, along with the only account from an observer invited to the shoot (the lucky writer was *American Cinematographer*'s editor, Herb Lightman). Even more far-reaching in its technical investigation was the sci-fi buffs' slick magazine *Cinefantastique*, whose 1978 issue on *Close Encounters* was rich and sometimes even recondite in its degree of nerdy detail. This extended coverage of *Close Encounters* was somewhat ironic: Frederick S. Clarke, the journal's curmudgeonly yet youthful founder, actively disliked *Close Encounters*, finding it lightweight compared to the deep speculations of his beloved *2001*. As Clarke put it in his Introduction to the issue:

> It gives me a great deal of pleasure to present this issue devoted to *Close Encounters of the Third Kind* for, despite my disappointment in the film as a whole, it is a milestone in the art of special visual effects. ... My problem with *Close Encounters of the Third Kind* is much the same as with *Star Wars*. They're both pretty much empty-headed. ... Spielberg's good-vibes star travelers, buzzing motorists in their UFOs, are the intellectual equivalent of the extraterrestrial barflies in *Star Wars*. ... For someone who so loved *2001: A Space Odyssey*, it's a shame Spielberg didn't tap Arthur C. Clarke or some other writer to work with.[35]

Frederick Clarke was transitioning *Cinefantastique* from extended critical interpretation (of his revered films) to technical, even geeky, accounts of the science that went into the making of science-fiction movies, and, to his mind, *Close Encounters* deserved attention in that respect. The movie clearly had marshalled vast assemblages of film-making craft, and that became the special issue's focus. Importantly, where Clarke disdained 'creatures in rubber masks doing cute things', for which he condemned both *Star Wars* and *Close Encounters*, the fabrication of the creatures is actually central to the special issue, as articles and interviews chronicle how Spielberg and his co-producers contracted a variety of speciality firms (crafting marionettes, electrically controlled figurines, sculpted faces, and so on), sometimes revising designs at the last minute and not always giving credit where due.

Predictably, special effects supervisor Douglas Trumbull received lots of attention in the magazines devoted to the technical aspects of the making of *Close Encounters*, even to the point that he is sometimes promoted as an alternative auteur to director Spielberg. As film scholar Scott Bukatman puts it in a canonic essay on Trumbull,

> While there are relatively few director-auteurs in SF film, cinematic style (as well as authorial consistency) can be located in the fields of art and effects direction. The special effects work of Douglas Trumbull is particularly distinctive and sustained in its evocation of the sublime. ... A Trumbull sequence is less the description of an object than the construction of an environment. ... Trumbull's work is especially contemplative. If he desires to create effects 'good enough to look at for a long period of time,' then his sequences have encouraged precisely this kind of activity.[36]

On *Close Encounters* Trumbull had his own effects lab near where Spielberg and editor Michael Kahn were working on their edit, so it was easy for Trumbull to track their progress and intervene quickly with his opticals. The hiring of Trumbull firmly

Douglas Trumbull

connects *Close Encounters* back to Kubrick's *2001* as Trumbull had pioneered the slit-screen psychedelics for that film's journey beyond consciousness. From *2001* into his effects efforts in the 1970s and beyond, Trumbull was driven by a research agenda to push effects-driven cinema to the maximum, even if this meant abandoning narrative for seemingly more sublime visual experience. Tying back to *2001* but also perhaps anticipating *Close Encounters*, early script versions of Trumbull's directorial debut, *Silent Running*, revealingly had themselves included consequential scenes of transcendental encounter with extraterrestrials.[37] While Trumbull was initially resistant to serve as hired hand on *Close Encounters*,

J. Allen Hynek

he concluded it was a good opportunity to advance his research on expanded spectacle.

Spielberg had initially conceived his idea for an alien encounters Hollywood movie as early as the beginning of the 1970s, discussing his premise with others in the New Hollywood orbit. An early working title was *Watch the Skies* (the last line of Howard Hawks's 1951 *The Thing from Another World*, a film cherished by Spielberg) and, after Watergate and other high-level governmental perfidy, Spielberg's primary focus became administrative cover-up of 'the UFO experience' (to quote the title of a book by J. Allen Hynek, originally an official debunker of UFO reports at the government's Project Blue Book but eventually converted into a true believer in close encounters).[38]

In an early career interview (the first in the volume *Steven Spielberg: Interviews*), Spielberg describes his next film after *Jaws* (i.e. *Close Encounters*, in pre-production at the time) as a 'political thriller' but immediately after terms it a 'science-fiction film'.[39] The slide is significant as over its narrative *Close Encounters* moves from one to the other, recounting how the government tries to control extraterrestrial visitations only to ultimately accept aliens as benign.

In the encounter with alien otherness and the concern with government cover-up, *Close Encounters* might seem to resemble Spielberg's previous film, *Jaws*, with which it is often paired for numerous reasons, including that these were big-budgeted, effects-driven box-office smashes that announced Spielberg as a master of mass-market entertainment.

Both films centre on initially beleaguered male protagonists who undertake quests that test their mettle. Along the way, these men resist conspiracy and team up with other folk (Sherriff Brody in *Jaws* with shark-hunter Quint [Robert Shaw] and scientist Hooper [Richard Dreyfuss], Roy with Jillian and and then with Lacombe's team), only in the final confrontation with creatures to be on their own. But here the resemblances end. Brody, of course, destroys the shark and then returns to civilisation as the credits roll, whereas Roy Neary goes on to a next stage of existence. Brody returns to the life he journeyed from and that now presumably has been cleansed of danger (until the sequels!) and, hopefully, of the government corruption that ignored, thereby enabling, the mounting threat. Of course, it matters that *Jaws*' shark stands as nothing but voracious menace, thus meriting annihilation. This is very different from *Close Encounters*, where certainly, as we have seen, the first encounters (especially at Jillian's isolated rural farmhouse) assume a degree of seeming menace but are subsequently washed away in the benign glow of the final encounter.

Whether or not the arrival of an inhuman Other in *Jaws* and *Close Encounters* portends danger or salvation, both films require belief in 'our' world as well as belief that credible forms of Otherness could intrude into it, even if not every spectator might really believe in visitation to 'our' world by UFOs in particular. (I employ the

possessive here since Hooper and Neary, played by the same actor, Richard Dreyfuss, are assumed as fictional characters to share 'our' time and 'our' geography – 1970s America). It is one small irony in the production history of the two movies that the craftspeople had significant trouble making a believable shark, while the special effects of *Close Encounters* easily work to foster faith in the extraterrestrials: before going to see *Jaws*, we know how sharks look and we certainly know that they exist in a realm adjacent to the human world; in contrast, we know little if nothing about outer-space aliens so the film-makers have latitude in their imaging and imagineering of the creatures.

Even as they start out in 'our' world, *Jaws* and *Close Encounters* already stylise that world towards fictional ends: a 'real' village represents island-town Amity in *Jaws*, but it's a select locale that fits a mythology of gingerbread picket-fence Americana along with quirky interiors like Quint's seaside shack. Likewise, the 'Muncie' of *Close Encounters* (actually, stand-in Mobile, Alabama) is a select vision of Middle America, a point made clear when Roy looks out at his suburban surroundings and absorbs it all as some kind of alien and alienating environment that he needs to repudiate.

As a kid, Spielberg had already made a *feature-length* UFO film, *Firelight* (1964), but a *Hollywood* feature was worlds apart, necessitating intensive financial negotiation and bureaucracy as much as technical craft, thus revolving centrally around deal-making as much as movie-making. While Spielberg obsessed early on about directing a Hollywood blow-up of his adolescent UFO film, he had to wait for *Jaws*' phenomenal success to get anyone even to listen to his pitch, let alone imagine putting his UFO idea into production.

Watch the Skies garnered its first influential support from Michael and Julia Phillips, who had turned to film producing from backgrounds, respectively, as a lawyer (and then Wall Street honcho) and as talent agent under David Begelman at Creative Management Associates (CMA). But perhaps as consequential as their production acumen, the Phillipses had a cool beach house that became a requisite

Julia and Michael Phillips

meeting point for the hip, newer Hollywood – from Dennis Hopper to John Milius to Paul Schrader, and on and on – a deal-making site along with a druggy party space. (Spielberg seems sometimes to have been in attendance but remained abstemious.) The Phillipses had served as line producers to bigwigs Richard Zanuck and David Brown, for a gambling and scamming story that would become the enormously successful *The Sting* (1973). After that film's big Oscars wins, Zanuck–Brown and the Phillipses went their separate ways, even as a variety of writers and directors continued to interweave between the two teams of producers: Zanuck and Brown began work on their shark movie, *Jaws*, with Spielberg eventually assigned as director, while the Phillipses produced Paul Schrader's script of *Taxi Driver*, with Martin Scorsese as director. Spielberg was keen to embark on a new project as *Jaws* entered into production (and then post-production), and the Phillipses optioned his UFO idea (now called *Close Encounters of the Third Kind*, from the typology of alien encounters that Hynek outlined in his book). They didn't want to deal with Zanuck–Brown again so brought it (after other studios demurred) to Columbia, where Julia's former CMA boss David Begelman was now studio head.

Columbia had experienced financial troubles early in the 1970s, including from under-performing films, and Begelman had been brought in (along with new company president Alan Hirschfield) to try to turn things around. Spiralling budgets needed to be reined in, but the success of Universal's *Jaws*, two years into the Begelman regime, made the prospect of a Spielberg project at Columbia exceptional and enticing.

It was logical for the Phillipses, having produced *Taxi Driver* from a Paul Schrader script, and knowing that Spielberg's initial premise involved government misdoings as experienced by one loner figure, to turn to Schrader for first draft screenplays. Almost fifty years on, it is not completely clear who did what and when in elaborating *Close Encounters*' story (including several other scriptwriters hired after Schrader): there are gaps in the archival records, problems of memory and issues of credit (Schrader wanted – and, it seems, still wants – his efforts acknowledged; Spielberg clearly felt it would strengthen his reputation as an auteur to be listed as sole writer [just as decades earlier Orson Welles had initially contemplated not sharing credit for the script of *Citizen Kane* (1941) with Herman J. Mankiewicz]).

Before honing the *Watch the Skies* premise into what he termed 'UFOs and Watergate' (as he formulated it around 1973 or 1974), Spielberg first seems to have imagined his 1970s UFO film as pretty similar to his teenage alien encounter film, *Firelight*: the new film was to start with a multi-faceted sociology of UFO visitation impacting a variety of Americans (revealingly, early in the 1970s he titled this cross-section view 'Experiences'). Yet, increasingly, the 'Watergate' aspects moved beyond ordinary Americans to focus on an authority figure who starts as a rational dis-believer, even an active de-bunker, yet comes after a close encounter of his own to be obsessed with aliens. As late as the 'making-of' documentary on DVD/Blu-ray editions of *Close Encounters*, Spielberg talks retrospectively of initially imagining his protagonist as either a policeman or a government official.

A curious document in this respect is a six-page *undated* set of notes, 'Close Encounters of the Third Kind: Preliminary Schemata', in the Paul Schrader papers at the University of Texas.[40] Essentially a tight plot outline, 'Preliminary Schemata' combines both premises that Spielberg bandied about when he first conceived the UFO project (that is, a cross-section of people who have 'Experiences' of aliens; concentration on one government de-bunker who converts to belief in UFOs). Like Spielberg's 'Experiences', the Schemata starts with an overview in which UFOs come ever closer to Earth, touching the lives of diverse small-town Americans (including couples in a lovers' lane, a motif from the much earlier *Firelight*). Here, in fact, it's worth remembering that even the eventual film of *Close Encounters* is not just about Roy Neary's visitation but that of Jillian, Barry, air traffic controllers, crowds in India, Middle Americans gathering at a knoll, and so on.

In this six-page outline, debunker turned believer Stoney Kelsum discovers not only that the government knows that UFOs exist but has for decades (since the Truman presidency) been communicating with aliens. With the help of another believer, Rand, Stoney breaks into a secret government facility ('maybe some gunplay', suggests the treatment) and learns when the next alien visitation will occur. Even though Rand sells out to the conspiracy, Stoney persists, arriving at what the outline terms a 'Stargate sequence. The revelation' as he runs towards the UFO he's dreamed of meeting up with.

In conversation with me, Paul Schrader did not remember this story outline (certainly not a protagonist named Stoney Kelsum), but he confirmed that the typeface was from his typewriter and employed wording that matched his typical phrasing (a dead giveaway: Kelsum's impactful encounter is titled 'The Road to Damascus', a fully Schraderian conceit). But it is quite possible that Schrader was simply taking ideas from Spielberg to spin them in his own fashion (Michael Phillips noted to me that no one works for Steven Spielberg without a lot of guidance!).

Two versions of Schrader's full screenplay exist, one in the archives, one online. Moving between the present, as scientists prepare for a major visitation by aliens, *and* events over the decades that prepared for this fateful encounter, Schrader's drafts centre on the spiritual journey of Air Force officer Paul VanOwen. Chronologically, the scripts start in 1960 when a small Indiana town, Clarenceville (not yet 'Muncie'), experiences a rash of UFO sightings, and VanOwen arrives to debunk the reports. When he has his own close encounter on the road back, he is himself mocked by higher-ups just as he had mocked everyday UFO believers. Falling into depression, becoming alienated from his wife and child, and guilt-ridden over his role in government conspiracy, VanOwen acquires new purpose when members of a secret government agency, Project Grief, ask him to join their operation, which is all about believing in UFOs and planning for further inevitable alien visitation. (In a curious anticipation of Roy Neary's question to Lacombe about the UFOlogist's covert operation, VanOwen initially asks one of the Project Grief men, 'Who are you guys?') VanOwen subsequently leaves his family to devote fully to Project Grief. Years into the operation, he decides the government project should try proactively to attract the UFOs back to Earth. Project Grief is renamed Project Entice, and the second script version pictures a UFO out in space watching developments and biding its time.

Much of that second script resembles the 'First draft', albeit with some significant additions. Like the eventual film of *Close Encounters* itself, Schrader's second script involves the military and its scientists, led by VanOwen, building a vast landing site in the hope of a return visit by aliens (anticipating here Lacombe in Spielberg's film). Moreover, as in the released film itself, the Project Entice team, to hide their operations from the public, spread word of a toxic waste disaster – a cover-up to get local populations away from the alien encounter staging site.

Notably, both scripts – but the second version more explicitly – continually depict VanOwen's interior revelations as essentially visions, implanted in him by the aliens, of all space and time, all memory of humanity within the cosmos overall, not just of his own physical close encounter. As the second script puts it, even in that encounter, 'the object VanOwen sees may not be real at all. It certainly is real to VanOwen, but from the evidence available we cannot be sure if it is a hallucination or a genuine close encounter.'[41] VanOwen very much develops into the sort of obsessive man, stuck in interior imaginings, so omnipresent in Paul Schrader's oeuvre.

As the originally Calvinist Schrader explains in the volume *Schrader on Schrader*, VanOwen's first name is an allusion to Saint Paul, initially a Pharisee persecutor of Christians who himself converted to Christianity after a visionary encounter with Christ on the Road to Damascus. ('Paul' is also, of course, Schrader's first name.) Interestingly, once Paul VanOwen has his vision and starts after elusive higher meaning, his turning against his former life includes walking out of a family church service when the priest starts to read from Saint Paul: Schrader has always had a complicated relationship with his own Christianity, and the implication in the church scene is that VanOwen is seeking a path to transcendence beyond any humanly organised formal religion (as Schrader himself was doing). At the end of his journey, Paul enters the alien spaceship but also burrows down into his soul and takes an ultimate mental trip, clearly inspired by *2001*: 'Paul has now plunged past the memory and the dream. He is exploring new worlds, achieving new knowledge, receiving sensations never before experienced by man. ... The Doors of Perception swing wide open.' And like *2001*, this script for *Close Encounters* then raises questions more than it offers answers: 'Is this what men dream of when they die? Is this the knowledge we pursue? Is this the heaven we seek?'[42]

An additional document now in the Schrader papers at the University of Texas at Austin titled 'Salient Points for a Revised Draft of *Close Encounters of the Third Kind*' (29 April 1974)[43] further complicates our understanding of who did what in developing the film's premise. Now, narrative motifs in these 'Salient Points' strongly anticipate elements in Spielberg's own scripts (and the released movie itself). The most striking development is Schrader's extended proposition that not merely should VanOwen 'continue to live with his family' after his UFO encounter (which, of course, Roy Neary attempts, only to discover how far he is alienated from them – and they, especially his wife, from him) but that while at home he undertakes 'unaccountable things', inspired by his close encounter, that closely resemble what happens in the film: 'digging up a tree … Hauling baskets of sand in from the field'. VanOwen, we are told, 'has removed the furniture, placed 6 inches of dirt over the carpet, built an irrigation system, planted grass arranged with stones and raked sand. … He knows there is some meaning in all this but he can't find it.' Again, nothing in the existing documentation confirms whether these new narrative developments came from conversations with Spielberg, yet it is striking that the notes already imagine VanOwen transforming interior home space into a built environment all the more unnatural from being cobbled together from natural objects like mud and uprooted shrubbery. The mountain that Roy Neary erects in his living room is one of the most impactful images in *Close Encounters*, and it is already there to a degree in the archived Schrader papers.

It is revealing that one document in Schrader's scant files on *Close Encounters* is a clipping from *The Hollywood Reporter* dated 22 April 1976, near the end of film production and long after Schrader's involvement had terminated. The short article notes that the budget has expanded from close to $3 million to over $11 million (it would later go much higher) but concentrates mostly on upcoming screenplay arbitration between Spielberg (and his producers) and Schrader and later, additional scriptwriter John Hill (whose draft, after Schrader's efforts, was also not used). Such arbitration was mandated given contracts the early-draft writers had signed, but the article hints strongly that neither Schrader nor Hill would pursue the case with any fervour as they accepted that what Spielberg had crafted was far removed in philosophy from their own imaginings about alien encounter. Schrader did realise, however, that if his name didn't appear in the film's credits, he wouldn't get any profit points, so he agreed to arbitration even as he asserted friendship with Spielberg and the Phillipses. Ultimately, though, the Writers Guild ruled that Schrader should not receive credit, solo or shared, for *Close Encounters of the Third Kind*.

In one version of why Schrader's scripts were rejected, the Phillipses evidently worried that the dark reputation of *Taxi Driver* might work against the upbeat fantasy of *Close Encounters*. Spielberg himself suggests strongly in his interview for the aforementioned special issue of *American Cinematographer* just at the film's release that he actually planned from the start to write the shooting script himself and employed writers like Schrader and John Hill primarily to get something to bounce his own ideas off. As he put it,

> I was originally going to write a screenplay, but I just did a treatment because *Jaws* came along. ... But in order to keep an idea fresh and exciting for me, I like to put somebody on it right away, even if it is not exactly what I want. It's nice to see a first trial and find out why it's not working ...'[44]

For what it's worth, Schrader himself offers a very different account, suggesting strongly that the differences were deeper, around conflicting imaginings of the protagonist and what he goes through on his quest and why:

> What I had done was to write this character with resonances of Lear and St. Paul, a kind of Shakespearean tragic hero, and Steven just could not get behind that ... I said, 'I refuse to send off to another world, as the first example of earth's intelligence, a man who wants to go and set up a McDonald's franchise,' and Steven said, 'That's exactly the guy I want to send.' Steven's Capra-like infatuation with the common man was diametrically opposed to my religious infatuation with the redeeming hero.[45]

Significantly, even though Schrader didn't get credit for *Close Encounters*, many of his premises, across his notes, script drafts and revision suggestions, remain in the film itself to echo concerns broadly on display in the New Hollywood of the early 1970s: failure of governance, paranoia, guilt, breakdown of family, personal identity driven by obsession (if not downright pathology), and so on.

Speaking to me just around the time of the release of Spielberg's autobiographical movie *The Fabelmans* (2022), Schrader offered this trenchant conclusion on his efforts to craft a *Close Encounters* screenplay (I paraphrase): 'I just yesterday finished adapting a Russell Banks story about a man dying of cancer. Spielberg just recently finished making a movie about a kid who likes making movies. That about sums it up.'[46]

In passing, it might be worth noting that, even if he was taken off *Close Encounters*, Schrader did get credit for another alienated-man screenplay the same year (although he claims this script ultimately was also drastically altered), the post-Vietnam vengeance drama *Rolling Thunder*. *Rolling Thunder*'s Charles Rane (William Devane) returns from years as a Vietnam POW, and he lives, like Travis Bickle in *Taxi Driver*, as a maladjusted loner who ultimately finds purpose, just like Bickle, in a murderous rampage in a bordello. (For Rane, it is about enacting vengeance against home intruders who killed his wife and son. In Schrader's comment on the two films, 'The main character in [*Rolling Thunder*] was meant to be the same sort of character, with that same social edge.') Like *Close Encounters*' Roy Neary, Charles Rane departs from home to an open-ended future. His last words after the carnage are to his war buddy who helped in the bloody massacre – 'Let's go home' – yet it is unclear what 'home' now means, since he has severed all ties to his pre-military home life. Unlike Neary, though, Blane actually seems to be heading nowhere spiritual, nowhere that offers redemption.

With previous screenwriters out of the picture, Spielberg took over the writing of *Close Encounters* and produced multiple screenplay drafts. The film itself would take up some elements from these scripts and drop others, and there were in fact modifications even to the final shooting script once on-set production began.

While these scripts didn't go so far as to realise Paul Schrader's sardonic image of the protagonist as a McDonald's franchisee, the biggest transformation, of course, was the decision to make the hero an ordinary working-class guy, and not a military expert. Significantly, though, institutional professionalism remains through the new character Lacombe, who essentially runs things from on high. Lacombe is given little backstory, but he brings a flexible sensitivity of character that offsets any conspiratorial quality. Notably, Spielberg's scripts assign an unconventional whimsy to his character by having his first meeting with Laughlin take place in a limousine at the airport where one of the flights that reported their close encounter to the air traffic controllers has just landed. Lacombe auditions Laughlin by having him translate pornography – to ensure that his translations convey emotions, since that may matter in any communication with aliens! (The scene was actually shot but deemed too static visually, and Spielberg substituted new footage of the meet-up, now in the striking opening sequence in the Sonora Desert, with its howling winds).

Most consequential, though, in fact was Spielberg's depiction of Roy Neary within a sociology of ordinary Middle Americanness. Like his earlier formulation, 'Experiences', Spielberg's scripts picture Neary as one suburbanite among many. For instance, his first draft opens with a quick anecdotal look at a night-time suburban street where all the neighbourhood dogs are barking desperately. A man emerges from one house, blasting a shotgun at the skies, and the dogs quiet down for a bit. Later, after Roy's close encounter, Ronnie and Roy attend a potluck block party, where the men and women divide up into gendered circles. While the men discuss the desirability of suburban conformity, Roy stares up at the sky and eventually everyone is distracted to do so, too. Ronnie becomes annoyed that Roy's behaviour is disrupting conventional neighbourhood life. (In the movie itself, Ronnie notes simply that all their friends are abandoning them because of Roy's behaviour.)

The scripts emphasise how Roy brings disturbance and difference into conventional or normative middle-class life. For instance, in a moment that thankfully was dropped, Roy, wanting comfort after Ronnie finds him crying in the bathroom, tries to initiate sex with her. But when he sees her bare breasts, his mountain vision returns and extinguishes his sexual urges!

Roy initially strives to adhere to a lifestyle appropriate to his demography but he quickly moves away from it. Roy Neary may not be a McDonald's franchisee but, in a telling detail, an early script scene has him driving along the fast-food commercial strip of Muncie to see if the lights are on before going to the countryside, where he quickly gets lost and has his fateful close encounter.

That encounter cuts Roy off from his present life. In one draft, when Roy impels his family back to the curve in the road where he and Jillian and others saw the UFOs, the scene ends with Ronnie asking him pointedly whether he'd go off with the UFOs if they returned, to which Roy emphatically says 'Yes'. Significantly, when Roy returns to the bend and encounters Jillian, their flirtatious banter gives him the confidence to ask her the same question: would she ever want to go off in one of the UFOs? In contrast to Roy's enthusiastic affirmation, Jillian admits she's not sure, perhaps setting up the released movie's ending where Roy goes off into outer space while Jillian watches approvingly, yet pointedly stays behind.

Portraits of the artist

'Monsieur Neary, êtes-vous un artiste, un peintre?'

Lacombe interrogating Roy Neary at Devils Tower
(Laughlin's translation: 'Mr Neary, are you an artist or a painter?')

At first glance, Richard Dreyfuss, an actor associated more with a New York liberal or creative milieu, might not seem to fit the role of a Midwest working-class guy likely to be sent out to check electricity lines. In *Jaws*, Dreyfuss is the East Coast egghead balanced against cop Brody and macho shark hunter Quint, and his class privilege, intellectual ambition and physical inadequacy all define his character (Quint claims Hooper's soft hands betray his 'wealthy college boy' background – to which Hooper replies in a way Neary likely never would, 'I don't need this "working-class hero crap"'). Neary's perhaps xenophobic exasperation at Lacombe, who, in Neary's words, 'isn't even an American', might fit the character but likely not the actor portraying him.

Yet, that Dreyfuss might not initially seem right as Roy Neary perhaps matches the narrative's sense that Neary himself is a kind of misfit: he's not the best working-class lineman around (he quickly gets lost); he's not the best suburban husband or father; he's not the best at accepting limited horizons, wondering instead if life holds some deeper meaning (the sort of spiritual questioning a New York intellectual might indulge in). In her short Spielberg biography for Yale's 'Jewish Lives' series, critic Molly Haskell even suggests that Dreyfuss's urban-intellectual Jewishness, never insisted on in his movies for Spielberg, may play into an outsider quality, the wandering figure hoping for a promised land beyond the home life he's already clearly alienated from in the first scenes.[47]

In the film that won Dreyfuss his Oscar the same year as *Close Encounters*, *The Goodbye Girl*, he is the archetypal artsy New Yorker, versed in the crafty ways of the big-city creative class. Yet, Roy Neary, nominally an electrical engineer at *Close Encounters*' outset, also becomes somewhat an artistic creator in his own right as the movie progresses (along with Jillian, whose original occupation [other than mother to Barry in a stereotype of the single mom] is never identified but seems art-related as she has a slew of painting brushes and easel). Roy and Jillian (along with Larry the Angeleno [Josef Sommer], who initially accompanies them up the mountain only to give up) are driven to externalise their inchoate yearnings *in works of art* – paintings, sketches and sculpture (and little Barry suddenly finds the talent to play the 'Close Encounters' theme on his xylophone). There's even the intimation that two-dimensional art like drawing fails to evoke the fullness of nature ('try sculpture',

Roy says to Jillian and Larry, whose art imagined only the front of Devils Tower), just as cinema mimics a rich roundness (especially in this enveloping movie, with sights and sounds that extend beyond the screen).[48]

An 'artist' with some of his oeuvre

Mountain images, big and small

As he sculpts mini-versions of the mountain vision deep in his mind, Roy laments that 'it's not right' and almost gives up. A frustrated tug reveals a butte that he stares at fixedly. He then turns his entire living room into a veritable set, directing, like a film director, his crew (his children) to help craft his larger-scale design. But the meaning is still not clear to him. One not so small irony is that, as he pants in frustration, mucky from his sculptural efforts, it's the mass art of small-screen television that reveals the visual splendour of what he hadn't caught in his art: the larger-than-life actuality of Devils Tower itself.

In a way, *Close Encounters* is concerned with the large-scale staging of visual spectacle – the aliens for the humans, but also the humans for the aliens. Within the film's narrative, just as in the making of a movie, there is: a 'staging area' (the term itself rendering the event as performance) – or several, since Roy's living-room mountain stands effectively as a DIY stage set; multiple levels of spectatorship (not only we viewers outside the film but also scientists and others within the storyworld); musical accompaniment; cameras rolling; and even applause. All this happens to the movie as movie, as well.

Insofar as *Close Encounters* references visual arts, especially the moving-image arts of film and television, the casting of François Truffaut as Lacombe makes sense, especially if we take the movie

Trying to direct

to be about the experience of cinema. For viewers who know his films (likely a small subset of *Close Encounters*' massive audience), Truffaut's performance as Lacombe brings with it connotations of cinematic artistry: he is a renowned French New Wave director, and his casting by Spielberg enables the movie to stand both as mass entertainment *and* an allusion to artistically ambitious cinema.

And it matters here that Truffaut comes to *Close Encounters* with the reputation of *director* more than actor. Throughout, whether yelling to masses in India or moving forcefully through a sandstorm, Truffaut's Lacombe 'directs' the operations he is involved in (and at times what Lacombe does within the fiction mimics what Spielberg had to do to orchestrate that fiction: for instance, both required large crews to handle that swarming crowd in India). In the film's finale, Lacombe is an observer like the others (he even has cameras rolling – it's all cinema), but he also attempts to organise the spectacle at hand. (Likewise, he serves as a sort of casting director when he 'auditions'

Roy on his readiness to join the outer-space enterprise and checks out Laughlin's French).

In an early academic study of *Close Encounters*, poet and literature professor B. H. Fairchild Jr cites Lacombe's assertion that if so many civilians felt impelled to journey to Devils Tower, it makes of their individual spiritual quests an 'event sociologique'. Nicely, Fairchild wonders whether this event is the shared sociology of spiritual quest within the film's storyworld or if 'it is Truffaut referring to the audience which has stood in line for hours to see *Close Encounters*'.[49] Yet, strikingly, Truffaut himself had earlier used the same phrase in a book on cinema to invoke what happens when lots of people assemble *for a film experience*: 'When a film achieves a certain amount of success, it becomes a sociological event and the question of its quality becomes secondary.'[50] The coincidence of Truffaut and Lacombe on this point is then also a blurring of what people *in the film* do in response to UFOs and what spectators *outside the film* do in watching (what Fairchild terms 'the film as film, rather than as mere ufology'[51]).

Yet the analogy of Lacombe to a director has its limits. Unlike, say, Spielberg (and crew), who tried to work out the complexities of story and special effects to the smallest detail (relying heavily on pre-visualisation storyboarding, albeit with some improvising during filming), Lacombe clearly cannot anticipate everything the aliens will do. He may 'direct' a battery of recording devices but they

Trying to direct

point towards an unpredictable reality (for example, any possible next moves by the aliens). Lacombe can 'direct' his musician (the man playing the synthesiser that 'talks' to the UFOs) to speed up the language of encounter ('plus vite, plus vite,' he demands), but he has no assurance of any response his commands might elicit (he implores the hovering UFOs: 'Allez, allez!'). His awestruck look is also a look of perplexity – peering out hopefully but unclear what will happen next.

Responses

Promotion for *Close Encounters* was both multi-pronged and minutely orchestrated. The pressbook, for instance, suggests local radio debates (about the existence or not of aliens) and displays at community planetariums or museums. It refers to a contest sponsored at the educational publication *Scholastic Magazine* to invite students to fashion questions for aliens and what they'd like to know about their planet. It promised to fly the winner (and his or her science teacher) to LA for a screening of the film, but I've found no evidence that this actually happened.

Yet a dire box-office fate for *Close Encounters* – and for Columbia itself – almost transpired when a financial writer for *New York* magazine, William Flanagan, snuck into one of the Dallas previews in October (Dallas was the location of a spectacularly successful preview for *Jaws* and Spielberg regarded the theatre he used for the screening there as a sort of talisman until a disastrous sneak preview for *1941* [1979]). Flanagan predicted, 'In my humble opinion the film will be a colossal flop.'[52] Flanagan's piece was loaded with snark, as in its dismissal of average movie-goers themselves for liking a film he found abysmal:

> Which leads me to conclude one of two things: When you give people free tickets to a movie, most of them are nice enough not to bitch [try telling that to the Pomona audience that in 1941 infamously torpedoed Orson Welles's *The Magnificent Ambersons*]. Or Texans see a lot of UFOs. R2-D2, where are you when we need you?[53]

Columbia stocks plummeted (so low that the New York Stock Exchange issued an emergency halt on trading), but that Flanagan's co-viewers greeted the film with such enthusiasm was the more telling factor: most viewers and most reviewers loved *Close Encounters*. For example, while she found it weak on character and depth, *New Yorker* critic Pauline Kael – so influential at the time in deciding which films urban professionals would find rewarding – was wowed by the movie's entertainment values:

> When it [the mother-ship] descends from on high, looming over the mountain and hovering there, no storybook illustration can compete with it. This is something only movies can do: dazzle you by sheer scale – and in this case by lights and music as well. *Close Encounters*, too, is a kids' movie in the best sense. ... Steven Spielberg is probably the most gifted American director who's dedicated to sheer entertainment.[54]

Close Encounters was a gigantic hit from the start and we can easily see it as an early case of the new sort of blockbuster that would dominate Hollywood cinema from then on: effects-driven and strong on spectacle, science-fictional or fantastic in its narrative premise, family-friendly, and so on.

In fact, those qualities both encouraged some negative comments on the film *and* made those comments economically irrelevant for a juggernaut of a movie that was for a while one of the biggest money-makers of all time (until other effects-driven blockbusters, including by Spielberg, soon followed). A particularly noteworthy critique came in renowned science-fiction writer Ursula K. Le Guin's virulent denunciation of *Close Encounters*, along with *Star Wars*, in a journal of spiritual investigation, *Parabola*. For Le Guin, *Close Encounters* was overblown, overdone (each effect overly signalled), over-loud (in a trenchant take-down, she termed the soundtrack an exercise in 'decibellicosity'), banal, gimmicky, 'grotesquely self-conscious', anachronistic (trafficking in outmoded religiosity long abandoned by legitimate science fiction), illogical, intellectually impoverished and a betrayal of the intellectual ambition of her chosen field of (literary) science fiction. As she put it,

> I was brought up to believe that science-fiction ... was supposed to try to be intellectually coherent, to have an idea and to follow it through. Neither of these movies would know an idea if they fell over it. ... Both are basically mindless.[55]

The movie's release pattern started with roadshow presentation (i.e. splashy special-event presentation in movie palaces) at just two theatres, New York's impressively cavernous Ziegfeld Theatre (where *2001* had itself famously roadshowed before general release) and LA's Cinerama Dome (which itself looks fairly futuristic, undoubtedly providing appropriate ambience for *Close Encounters*).

Fortuitously, I have a witness to the original roadshow who can attest to just how essential *Close Encounters* was perceived to be by audiences in advance of its release, and how much the film, when presented big, lived up to that anticipation.

Ken Sweeney, the lead administrator of my academic department, the Martin Scorsese Department of Cinema Studies, at NYU, was a 12-year-old boy growing up in Providence, Rhode Island, and fascinated, like so many other kids, by splashy Hollywood films. Ken had an aunt living in New York City, and the family would undertake road trips there for Broadway shows and movie-palace film screenings. As Ken recounts, he was especially eager to make the trip for *Close Encounters*: like so many other avid movie-goers in the mid-1970s, he had already seen and loved *Jaws* and was intrigued by director Spielberg, but also *Close Encounters* promised so much in the way of spectacular science fiction:

> I had seen *Jaws* the day after it opened, and several times that summer. I already knew Steve from many TV reruns of his *Night Gallery* and *Duel* – those were really popular with elementary kids in the early 70s ... *Close Encounters* was a film that made me very happy, I suspect because I was obsessed with

UFOs when I was in late elementary into junior high and found a copy of that crazy book *Chariots of the Gods* [a bestseller about alien visitations throughout history]. Also, all my friends were obsessed with that wacky Leonard Nimoy show *In Search of* ... which covered every scary thing from Big Foot to the Bermuda Triangle every week, and we thought it was gospel.[56]

Actually, *Close Encounters* did not have all the formal traits of the famous roadshow movies of the 1960s such as *2001* or *Lawrence of Arabia* (1962) (a film much beloved by Spielberg and perhaps alluded to in *Close Encounters*' opening where the blast of music over the sand-swept desert seems to echo Maurice Jarre's symphonic theme for *Lawrence* announcing an editing leap into the desert): it was not long enough to have an intermission (although it was, at 135 minutes, longer than many regular features in the period), and the roadshow theatre did not offer advance tickets *with assigned seating*. (In fact, the Sweeney family ended up in the *front* row.) But opening in exclusive, spectacular venues like the Ziegfeld or the Dome gave *Close Encounters* the impression of prestige, and its international locations and cast (numbering, in the India sequence, into the hundreds), and a vast sweep of history (the 1970s present/the 1940s past), do echo features of the traditional roadshow. Notably, like the celebrated blockbusters of the 1960s, tickets to the *Close Encounters* roadshow came with a multi-page souvenir programme.

Ken's family planned to see the film on the Saturday after Thanksgiving, but it had already been selling out early every morning for all of each day's screenings. So early on Sunday, as a major snowfall hit the city, Ken's family got in line (already stretching around the block) as early as possible, each member taking turns ducking into a nearby hotel to warm up from the cold. Finally, after hours of waiting, the line moved forward and the family snagged a ticket – for 5 p.m. This meant getting back on the road at around 8 p.m. for the four-hour or more drive back to Providence in what was now a blizzard. The kids bubbled in the back while the parents up front squabbled for much of the drive. As Ken recounts, 'Lots of arguing all the way up 95 north and a nasty, passive aggressive dinner at HoJos in Darien that I remember quite well, as my already angry dad swatted me for building Devils Tower out of sugar packets at the table.'[57]

The Sweeney family's experience is likely not that atypical in a period where blockbusters were must-sees that gained in value the earlier they were viewed in the film's run, and where, increasingly, giving up a day (into the night) for the experience was not unheard of. Maybe there's something a bit extraordinary in the idea of driving from Rhode Island to New York to see a mass entertainment, but it also has its anodyne qualities: just as the Neary parents scour the newspaper for a movie to take the family to, real-life families in the 1970s became increasingly invested in entertainment that everyone could participate in – and maybe *had* to participate in. In other words, to echo Claude Lacombe, 'an event sociologique'.

Spin-offs, ancillary items and 'sequels'

Interestingly, there is little direct product placement in *Close Encounters*. It is a film that is suspicious of all the commodities that fill up Middle American suburban lives. There's the McDonald's where the alien-induced blackout of Muncie begins: within the crushing blandness of Muncie, which becomes ever more intolerable to Roy Neary, that a franchise fast-food restaurant loses power

McDonald's about to have a close encounter

is a mark maybe of the worthlessness of commodity culture. There are also the trucks bearing the names of national product manufacturers (Baskin-Robbins, for example), but there the reference is even potentially more critical: the trucks are fakes, meant to hide government investigation of the UFO phenomenon, so there's the suggestion that beneath consumerism lies the conspiratorial. There is also a lot of Budweiser beer (open cans lying around, ads on TV) in Roy Neary's working-class home before he abandons it. In this respect, it matters that while product placement runs through movie history, it was actually in 1976 and 1977, just around the time of *Close Encounters*, that the two top firms devoted to orchestrating contact between movie studios and product manufacturers began operation: in other words, *Close Encounters* was in production and then release just when newly modernised forms of product placement were developing, and the movie might have come too early for the full articulation of the product-placement phenomenon.

It's rather in the realm of tie-ins – consumer items that reference *Close Encounters* – that product marketing really took off. The latter part of the 1970s saw the ancillary markets for tie-ins explode, as blockbusters seemed to push consumers to want the big-screen experience extended through domestic possessions, and *Close Encounters* seemed tailor-made for tie-in marketing. Given the continuities we've seen between the earlier downbeat New Hollywood films and later blockbusters, *and* the differences between them, it might be silly to note the obvious: a film of everyday alienation like, say, *Five Easy Pieces* wouldn't have generated a Bobby Dupea action figure, but the later movies, so centred theatrically on sensation and visual spectacle, easily spun off into products that continued the experience. There might not be an action figure for the battered and bloodied, but repentant, Travolta on his subway ride at the end of *Saturday Night Fever*, but, unsullied, his outfit could contribute to a fashion-conscious cultural moment, along with its kinetic Bee Gees score (which generated one of the most successful tie-in LPs of all time).

Saturday Night Fever (1977): an inaction figure?

The vast array of tie-ins for *Close Encounters* confirms just how much this fantasy blockbuster departed from earlier earthbound New Hollywood films of an alienated man desperate for meaning in life *and* moved away from gritty realism. While some tie-ins sought to adapt the filmic *narrative* to other media – for instance, a photo-novel, a Marvel comic book and a novelisation attributed to Spielberg himself (but ghost-written) – most of them concentrate predictably on a striking visual moment or iconic scene. Many skew towards younger consumers, extending the movie experience through play: for example, a jigsaw puzzle, a board game, trading cards (including some with membership forms for the 'CE3K Skywatchers' club inserted into packets of that all-American commodity Wonder Bread), detachable postcards, a Mattel model of Roy's truck, a pinball machine, a lunchbox with thermos (now much beloved by collectors) and, of course, figurines (some pliant) of space aliens.

It is perhaps telling that of the forty-eight offerings in the postcard set, *none* show Roy Neary, whereas Jillian (and Barry) gets a few cards. Perhaps they were deemed more visually quotable because of just how visceral and sensational the two visits by spaceships to their home turn out to be. True, the first close encounter that Roy

Solving the puzzle of the cosmos (courtesy Andrew Sheppard)

has with the aliens, in his truck along a railroad track, is spectacular, but the dazzling burst of lights, along with zero-gravity propulsion of items from the glove compartment, happens visually to the vehicle as much as to the man inside. (Moreover, as noted, the truck does get its tie-in maybe because trucks are kid collectibles and, to a degree, suggests a dynamism not so different from that of speeding UFOs – as we see when Roy chases them through a toll booth separating Indiana and Ohio).

Evidently, Dreyfuss had become enough of a star to dictate when and where his likeness could be used, and he didn't want to appear in trading cards and suchlike (the Marvel comic substitutes a pretty hunky He-Man like those that populate macho-action cinema from *Rocky* [1976] and *First Blood* [1982] on). Truth be told, though, except for some moments of alienated weirdness like fashioning Devils Tower models from mashed potatoes or, on a larger scale, from mud and uprooted plants and detritus that take over his living room, Roy is not that visually dynamic but often ineffectual or passive – crying while immersed fully clothed in his bathtub –

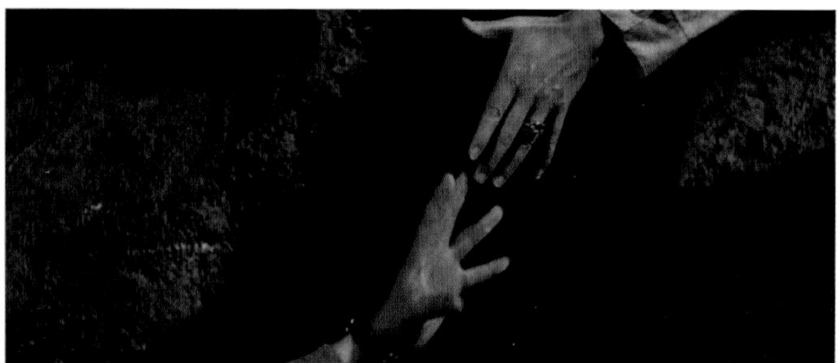

Northwesterly hands

or pleading pathetically for acceptance (of himself, of his visions). Even when, by resolute will, he makes it to Devils Tower, Roy is still more of a bumbler than an action hero – for example, slipping dangerously as he tries to climb to the other side of the Tower and needing Jillian's outstretched hand to help him, an allusive gender reversal of a late scene in *North by Northwest* (1959), just before a loudspeaker announces that the aliens are approaching from 'north northwest', making the allusion explicit. Roy's not really a visually vibrant heroic figure of the sort that lends itself to figurines or trading cards. The muscular hero, to take the example of Sylvester Stallone in the films cited above, seems much more appropriate a source of visually dynamic tie-in (including not only figurines but also, in the case of *First Blood*, the big knife the big man uses).

While *Close Encounters* resembles blockbuster franchises of the moment in its array of tie-ins, one obvious way in which the movie doesn't fit is in the absence of a *sequel*. Obviously, there could be no direct narrative sequel to *Close Encounters* without betraying the un-closed ending in which Roy heads off to an unseen future. Even when Spielberg received funds to shoot new footage inside the UFO (along with material closer to his own heart), the added scene can't close Roy's story in a manner that would easily enable a sequel.

Instead, it seems that early on there were plans to develop a new film that would forego Roy's chronicle in favour of the alien encounters of other earthlings. In fact, several times in his extended interview in the aforementioned 'Making-of' issue of *Cinefantastique*, appearing just after *Close Encounters*' release, Spielberg was emphatic that he was imagining a sequel, albeit quite reluctant to offer any details.

After Lawrence Kasdan turned down an invitation to write the follow-up, Spielberg, a fan of Joe Dante's early exploitation horror film *Piranha* (1978) (a clear parody of *Jaws*), commissioned that film's screenwriter, John Sayles, to draft an alien encounter story. With the working title *Night Skies*, Sayles's script offers a bifurcated narrative around alien visitation: on the one hand, fearsome aliens leave a horrific trail of mutilated cows (they are dissecting Earth creatures as they search for our planet's top beings), and here the story renders the space creatures quite menacing in line with outer-space monster-invasion movies of the 1950s (the script loosely takes inspiration from a supposed close encounter from that decade); on the other hand, one of the aliens is a benevolent creature who bonds with an autistic adolescent loner.[58]

Columbia put the project on hold while Spielberg worked for Paramount on *Raiders of the Lost Ark* (1981), and next on a film owed to Universal. The project was eventually dropped but Spielberg would, of course, revive the theme of a loner boy bonding with an alien in 1982's *E.T.*, and he later produced Joe Dante's *Gremlins* (1984), which in its own fashion picks up on the split in *Night Skies* between a good creature and a bad, albeit not outer-space monsters but earthly beings with supernatural origins.

Increasingly, after the release of *Jaws 2* (1978 – one year after *Close Encounters*, that is) – which did well at the box office but had no involvement from Spielberg, who in fact reviled it – Spielberg talked *against* the idea of a sequel to *Close Encounters*. Instead, as noted, he worked on new versions of the movie itself, shooting additional footage, incorporating deleted scenes and removing some material.

Altogether, there are three different 'official' versions of *Close Encounters*: the original theatrical release (135 minutes),

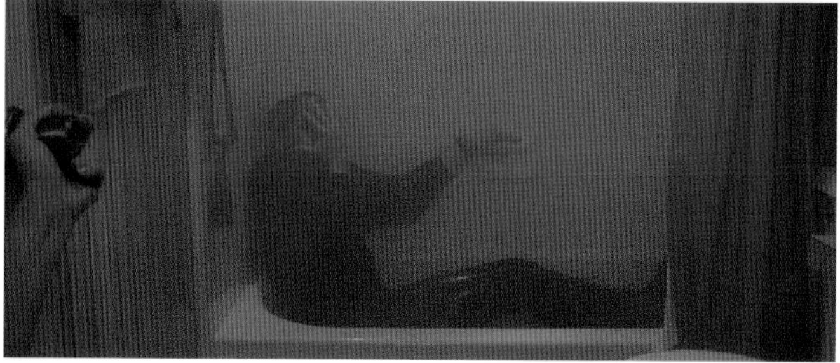

Power station scene, cut in later releases (Special Edition); bathtub meltdown scene, added to later releases (Director's Cut)

followed in 1980 by the so-called Special Edition (132 minutes) and then a 'Director's Cut' (137 minutes). As noted, the Special Edition originated from the studio wanting more footage of Roy *inside* the mother-ship, although Spielberg also took advantage of the studio entreaty to add new footage (in particular, the Gobi Desert sequence, more family dynamics in the Neary home) *and* to cut out some scenes (notably, the power station sequence where Roy gets sent out on the road and, most curiously, the impactful scene of Roy ransacking the neighbourhood for his large-scale living-room mountain). Few viewers liked the extended non-ending, so it was dropped when Spielberg re-released the Director's Cut (1997). This version continued to leave out the power station sequence, but otherwise it was essentially a compilation of best scenes from the first two cuts.

Continuing encounters with *Close Encounters*

Located almost where East Greenwich Village hits the Lower East Side, Anthology Film Archives is a venerable institution focused intently on the non-venerable and the non-institutional – an art temple (in virtually spiritual terms) for experimental non-narrative, the outré and the outlier, punky DIY, and overwhelmingly anti-Hollywood, especially in its big blockbuster storytelling modes. Somewhat surprising, then, to find that, in mid-November 2022, Anthology was screening an original 35mm print of *Close Encounters*. However, the choice ultimately made some sense as it was part of a series entitled 'Watch the Skies: UFOlogy on Screen' ('Watch the skies' was one of the advertising slogans for *Close Encounters* and, as noted, an early working title). As Anthology publicity explained, the series

> considers an array of films and videos … from underground videotapes to Hollywood blockbusters, and encompassing the stories of motley characters from contactees, renegade scientists, and New Age mystics to conspiracy cranks and shifty opportunists. … fleeting lights in the night skies and the obsessives drawn to making sense of them.

Of *Close Encounters*, it noted, 'Despite its Hollywood pedigree and humanist touch, it remains one of the most diligently faithful screen translations of UFO research.'

In fact, the short that preceded *Close Encounters*, Cauleen Smith's *H-E-L-L-O* (2014), fit more with Anthology's typical screening choices (to the extent that anything is typical about Anthology's non-normative programming): *H-E-L-L-O* is an eleven-minute non-narrative depiction of street musicians in New Orleans, each playing part or all of the *Close Encounters* five-note theme, sometimes accompanied by slow camera movement, sometimes not. As an experimental work, *H-E-L-L-O* eschews story for a street realism from which grows the transcendental – the city's everyday byways as sites for sheer musicality. Of course, these are not streets from just any place: for a city devastated nine years earlier by floods,

H-E-L-L-O evokes how musical inspiration can sustain communities. Yet, while the aural motif from *Close Encounters* offers iconic recognisability, there is irony perhaps in referencing a blockbuster about a man who goes his own rebellious way, to celebrate collective spirit within a challenged city.

In fact, the lead-in to the screening itself tried hard to dispel any Hollywood aura. The two films were introduced by an author on cult phenomena (and Anthology is itself pretty cultish). In black studded leather with chains, and sporting somewhat punky hair, the presenter seemed to go out of his way not to talk of *Close Encounters* as a 'Spielberg' film: he focused instead on how the movie tapped into UFOlogy and asserted how Lacombe was based on real UFOlogist Jacques Vallée, who developed, the speaker explained, 'the interdimensional hypothesis' (which, it seems, asserts that extraterrestrials arrive not physically but as mental forces that somehow implant visions in us – almost a throwback to Paul Schrader's scripts with their sense of spiritual interiority).

Whatever brought so many people to Anthology that night, I at least was there to watch *Close Encounters* large-screen on celluloid – a format I'd not seen it in since its original release. That also seemed to be the motivation for the young man next to me in line (we were the first ones there). Trevor, it transpired, worked at a documentary film non-profit in Brooklyn but had cinephile interest in all sorts of films. He knew many of Spielberg's movies well but had never seen *Close Encounters* and was eager to do so on a big screen. Later, Trevor described his reactions in an email (his youthful response bears comparison to the earlier recollection of administrative director Ken when he saw it in 1977):

> I didn't know much about it beforehand – only murmurings from friends and folks at screenings of other films (classic, aliens, Spielberg, visually impressive) ... One big driving factor was the unique opportunity to see an old film in a theater ... Bolstered by the fact that it was a Spielberg film. ... Spielberg's name had a bit more of an effect on me than I think it normally would have.

> I was pleasantly surprised by how much of an emotional effect the characters' experiences had on me. … I found myself contemplating what it is like to be perceived as an outsider, even a lunatic, but found great relief when the characters were vindicated in their beliefs. Then, there's just this great story of humans having a *peaceful* interaction with an extraterrestrial species.[59]

Trevor's response is obviously only one subjective bit of evidence, yet we can add it to accounts I've cited throughout of other viewings – from 1970s critics to spectators today, young and older, male and female. Noteworthy is that virtually everyone cites the special effects, confirming that they more or less 'held up' – even Ursula K. Le Guin, in her critique of the film, acknowledged begrudgingly that for her the problem was indeed their overwhelming effectiveness. Maybe that's what makes the movie worthy of critical analysis decades after its release: that the effects are so good, so 'realistic', they give its story of an alienated man searching for happiness against domestic responsibility an air of possibility and believability. Today, the movie's tale crashes up against the real world, where we are necessarily critical of the centredness of mass-culture narratives on *men* finding their way. *Close Encounters* stages its story with verve and imagistic force that makes it a movie worth returning to, worth engaging with.

'Man's fate'

Notes

1 Richard Combs, 'Primal Scream: An Interview with Steven Spielberg' (1977), in Lester D. Friedman and Brent Notbohm (eds), *Steven Spielberg: Interviews* (Jackson: University Press of Mississippi, 2000), p. 33.
2 Robert S. Lynd and Helen Merrell Lynd, *Middletown: A Study in Modern American Culture* (New York: Harcourt Brace and Company, 1929), p. 117.
3 Spielberg's own scripts as well as the novelisation make the sexual overtones explicit. In the novel's words: '[Jillian] opened her blouse to reveal the upper curve of her breasts … She watched as Roy's cheeks turned a shade darker. "I'm sorry," she said, buttoning up. "I just had the feeling you were my oldest friend."' Steven Spielberg, *Close Encounters of the Third Kind* (New York: Dell, 1977), p. 97. (The volume was actually ghost-written by Leslie Waller, well known in the 1970s as a go-to person for such novelisations.)
4 Peter Krämer suggests insightfully that E.T. from 1982 sort of *is* that sequel: a clueless single mom left with three children after the husband has gone off, all of them dealing fitfully with the abandonment. Email to author from Peter Krämer, 23 April 2023.
5 Julia Phillips, *You'll Never Eat Lunch in This Town Again* (New York: Random House, 1991), p. 149.
6 Bradley Schauer, *Escape Velocity: American Science Fiction Film, 1950–1982* (Middletown, CT: Wesleyan University Press, 2017).
7 A pointed exception is the George Roy Hill adaptation from 1972 of Kurt Vonnegut's novel *Slaughterhouse-Five*. While earthlings Billy Pilgrim and Montana Wildhack are indeed spirited away to an alien planet for observation and experimentation, the movie stands as a quirky one-off dramatic fantasy that tries to find filmic parallels with the cult novel.
8 Julie Turnock offers a perceptive analysis of the continuities in visual style between early Seventies street gritty New Hollywood and later effects-driven blockbusters in *Plastic Reality: Special Effects, Technology, and the Emergence of 1970s Blockbuster Aesthetics* (New York: Columbia University Press, 2015). Chapter 6, '"More Philosophical Grey Matter": The Production of *Close Encounters of the Third Kind*' (pp. 179–99), deals closely with Spielberg's movie.
9 Schauer, *Escape Velocity*, p. 8.
10 Vivian Sobchack, *The Limits of Infinity: The American Science Fiction Film, 1950–1975* (South Brunswick, NJ, and New York: A. S. Barnes, 1980); *Screening Space: The American Science Fiction Film* (New York: Ungar Press, 1987; rpt., Rutgers University Press, 1997).
11 On a side note, it is an intriguing detail that the music earthlings craft in order to 'talk' to aliens is *computer-generated*. Scientific engineering has its role to play but only as a step to something higher, beyond science, beyond technology. In a charming YouTube clip labelled 'Best interview question', famed movie interviewer James Lipton gets Spielberg's heartfelt approbation when he suggests that the combination of computer and music echoes Spielberg's own autobiography, caught as he was between a father

who designed computers and a mother who loved music (a combination later explored in *The Fabelmans* [2022]). Available at: <https://www.youtube.com/watch?v=g6lcT4EhNzM> (accessed 24 January 2024).

12 It's not only in Spielberg films that we find the ominous or awed look off screen. William Friedkin's *Sorcerer*, from the same year as *Close Encounters*, has a lengthy example of the off-screen look when the scruffy band of misfits and losers delivering dynamite to a mining camp encounter something daunting beyond the frame and stare and stare and stare: eventually, a cut reveals that there is a massive uprooted tree blocking their path. That *Sorcerer* attempts to build on Roy Scheider's growing star reputation after *Jaws* perhaps links Friedkin's film to Spielbergian influences.

13 'Gene Siskel Interviews Steven Spielberg', in Roger Ebert and Gene Siskel, *The Future of the Movies: Interviews with Martin Scorsese, Steven Spielberg, and George Lucas* (Kansas City, MO: Andrews McMeel/Buena Vista, 1991), p. 72.

14 Joseph McBride, *Steven Spielberg: A Biography* (Jackson: University Press of Mississippi, 2010), p. 17.

15 Quoted in Thomas Durwood, *Close Encounters of the Third Kind: A Document of the Film* (Kansas City, MO: Ariel Books, 1977), p. 36.

16 Sam Kellogg, as of this writing a doctoral candidate in the Media, Culture and Communication Department at NYU, whose dissertation covers media representations of wilderness sites in national parks, offered by email this useful background (10 July 2023): Devils Tower, he explains,

> known as Mato Tipila, or Bear Lodge, to the Lakota, is an incredibly sacred and significant place to a number of Indigenous peoples – a place of reverence. Mountains have figured as places of power and encounter with the sacred or supernatural in many cultures, and so the choice of Mato Tipila as a setting for humanity's contact with an alien presence in the film could be understood as tapping in to one or another sacred mountain tradition, but also as a conspicuous erasure of existing native relations and beliefs (which long predate more recent attention from geologists, conspiracy theorists, rock climbers, and tourists). … Point being, this is a place where there's a lot of intense believing and witnessing and encountering happening in different, often incompatible ways: a symbolically loaded site for the movie to climax.

In *Alternate Americas: Science Fiction and American Culture*, M. Keith Booker astutely notes two oddities in the television broadcast that enables Roy Neary (with a cross-cut to Jillian also viewing the same news show) to identify Devils Tower as the mountain he's had obsessively in his mind: the TV commentator says Devils Tower was 'the first national monument erected in this country' (as if it were a human structure); and the announcer gets the date of its dedication by Theodore Roosevelt wrong (putting it as 1917, not 1906).

For Booker, these strange errors might fit in with the film's critique of mass television, among other lowbrow forms of popular culture. See Booker, *Alternate Americas* (Westport, CT: Praeger, 2006), p. 136.

17 Dan North, 'The Spielberg Effects', in Nigel Morris (ed.), *A Companion to Steven Spielberg* (Hoboken, NJ: John Wiley & Sons, 2017), p. 379.

18 In much Seventies American cinema (and after), helicopters immediately signal menace – a cold technology that sweeps and swoops down to track people and keep them in line. See, for instance, Joseph Losey's 1970 *Figures in a Landscape*, a very allegorical investigation of the fight for freedom, with the helicopter standing in for the evils of militarised modernity. As one history of the helicopter's cultural symbolism puts it:

> [T]he autonomous 'hermetic helicopter' is sleek and dark-canopied, self-contained and sealed, with no openings to the world, as if it were an alien spacecraft. In this guise, the helicopter further symbolises Vietnam brought home in the threatening tendencies of technology and state control – the wire-taps, Pentagon Papers and Watergate lies bred by the war.

(Alasdair Spark, 'Flight Controls: The Social History of the Helicopter as a Symbol of Vietnam', in Jeffrey Walsh and James Aulich [eds], *Vietnam Images: War and Representation* [New York: Palgrave Macmillan, 1989], p. 104.) Even as the successive scripts for *Close Encounters* moved away from the focus on government cover-up – and even as the course of the film comes benignly to leave military venture behind (back on the facing side of Devils Tower), the movie gains much socio-political resonance from the iconography of the helicopter as fearful, mechanised disciplining of recalcitrant populations.

19 Sobchack, *The Limits of Infinity*, p. 284.

20 A useful analysis of the film's music, especially its flirtations with an atonality that ultimately cedes to melodic user-friendly nostalgia, is Neil Lerner, 'Nostalgia, Masculinist Discourse and Authoritarianism in John Williams's Scores for *Star Wars* and *Close Encounters of the Third Kind*', in Philip Hayward (ed.), *Off the Planet: Music, Sound and Science Fiction Cinema* (Eastleigh, Hants: John Libbey Publishing, 2004), pp. 96–108. Lerner asserts that *Close Encounters* enacts

> Spielberg's seemingly inevitable movement from cues with a pointed lack of melody early in the film [...] to later cues featuring a clear, familiar melodic theme ... The score thus sets up the more experimental musical style as strange by associating it with the aliens, and ultimately it rejects this modernist, musical language, substituting tonality for atonality. (p. 102)

21 Frank Warner, 'The Sounds of Silence and Things That Go "Flash" in the Night', *American Cinematographer* 59, no. 1 (January 1978), pp. 44–5.

22 See Chuck Austin, '*Close Encounters of the Third Kind*: Director Steve Spielberg', *Filmmakers Newsletter* 11, no. 2 (December 1977), p. 30.

23 Michael Coates identifies the chosen format for numerous theatres at his Digital Bits website. Available at: <https://thedigitalbits.com/columns/history-legacy-showmanship/ce3k-40th/page-2>.
24 Warner, 'The Sounds of Silence', pp. 92–3.
25 Bill Whittington, *Sound Design & Science Fiction* (Austin: University of Texas Press, 2007), p. 122.
26 Email to author from Gianluca Sergi, 10 March 2023.
27 For Sergi's fuller history of Dolby Stereo in the 1970s, see his canonic *The Dolby Era: Film Sound in Contemporary Hollywood* (Manchester: Manchester University Press, 2006).
28 In a sardonic comment on box-office obsession around a later Spielberg blockbuster (*Jurassic Park* [1993]), critic Stuart Klawans wonders:

> Is any of that money headed toward *my* bank account? But perhaps I've missed the point. From the tone of the news report, I can tell that *Jurassic Park*'s success must surely be my success, too. As if in a potlatch, I can participate in the communal good fortune by offering my $7.50 to the next week's gross. To quote the ad campaign, 'Be a Part of Motion Picture History!' What a joy all of America must feel, as the numbers rise higher and higher!

(Klawans review in *The Nation* [19 July 1993], quoted in McBride, *Steven Spielberg: A Biography*, p. 424.)
29 Quentin Tarantino, *Cinema Speculation* (New York: HarperCollins, 2022), p. 287.
30 Ray Bradbury, 'Introduction', in Thomas Durwood (ed.), *Close Encounters of the Third Kind: A Document of the Film* (New York: Columbia Pictures, 1977), p. 14.
31 As producer Michael Phillips puts it, '[Spielberg] decided to make sure the ending was so loaded. It was a cornucopia. … Every time you think, "This is enough. If the movie ends here, I'm satisfied," he comes out with more.' Interview with Luke Ford, 'Michael Phillips Still Eats Lunch in This Town' (2002). Available at: <https://www.lukeford.net/profiles/profiles/michael_phillips.htm> (accessed 24 January 2024).
32 See, among other analyses, the canonic study by Andrew Britton, 'Blissing Out: The Politics of Reaganite Entertainment', *Movie* nos. 31–2 (1986), pp. 1–42.
33 For a fine study of Schrader, see George Kouvaros, *Paul Schrader* (Urbana: University of Illinois Press, 2008). From the same historical moment, meriting comparison to Schrader right down to the casting of Harvey Keitel in their first films as directors, is another screenwriter of obsessive masculinity on the edge, James Toback, with his script for Karel Reisz's 1974 *The Gambler* and then his directorial debut in 1978, *Fingers*. See Adrian Martin, 'Grim Fascination: Fingers, James Toback, and 1970s American Cinema', in Thomas Elsaesser, Alexander Horwath and Noel King (eds), *The Last Great American Picture Show: New Hollywood Cinema in the 1970s* (Amsterdam: Amsterdam University Press, 2004), pp. 309–31.

34 Ray Morton, *Close Encounters of the Third Kind: The Making of Steven Spielberg's Classic Film* (New York: Applause Theatre and Cinema Books, 2007); Michael Klastorin, *Close Encounters of the Third Kind: The Ultimate Visual History* (New York: Columbia Pictures/ HarperCollins, 2017); Bob Balaban, *Close Encounters of the Third Kind Diary* (New York: Paradise Press, 1978). There are also 'Making-of' documentaries on various DVD/Blu-rays of the movie. Additionally, Julia Phillips's infamous (and not always trustworthy) memoir *You'll Never Eat Lunch in This Town Again*, published around ten years before her sad death from cancer, discusses in passing the shoot for *Close Encounters*. And critic Jon Towlson provides useful background information, especially around the movies that inspired Spielberg, above all from Ford, Capra and Hitchcock, in his concise *Constellations: Studies in Science Fiction Film and TV* volume on *Close Encounters* (Leighton Buzzard, Beds: Auteur Books, 2016). Most recently, there is a tight overview of the film in Laurent Bouzereau's large-format celebration, *Spielberg: The First Ten Years* (San Rafael, CA: Insight Editions, 2023), pp. 120–55.
35 Frederick S. Clarke, 'Sense of Wonder', *Cinefantastique* 7, nos. 3–4 (Winter 1978), p. 3.
36 Scott Bukatman, 'The Artificial Infinite: On Special Effects and the Sublime', *Matters of Gravity: Special Effects & Supermen in the 20th Century* (Durham, NC: Duke University Press, 2003), pp. 82, 94, 95.
37 On alien encounter in *Silent Running*, see Mark Kermode's sharp BFI Film Classic on the film (2014).
38 Spielberg's film both takes direct inspiration from Hynek's book *and* diverges from it in one major way: on the one hand, the scene of air traffic controllers communicating with commercial pilots up in the air borrows many elements from Hynek in his account of radar close encounter (down to the ultimate decision by the pilots not to report a UFO sighting); on the other hand, Hynek pointedly excludes *contact with aliens* from his notion of a 'close encounter of the third kind'. For Hynek, it is all too easy for reports of such contact to be dismissed as coming from kooks or cranks, so he tries to avoid any expressed acceptance of his own of 'contactee' accounts. See J. Allen Hynek, *The UFO Experience: A Scientific Inquiry* (New York: Ballantine Books, 1972).
39 'At Sea with Steven Spielberg' (1974 interview by David Helpern in *Take One*), in Friedman and Notbohm (eds), *Steven Spielberg: Interviews*, p. 15.
40 Paul Schrader Papers, Harry Ransom Library Archives, University of Texas, Series 1, Container 27.3.
41 Paul Schrader, 'Close Encounters of the Third Kind', second script draft. Available at: <https://thescriptsavant.com/movies/Close_Encounters_Of_The_Third_Kind.pdf> (accessed 24 January 2024), p. 36.
42 Ibid., pp. 130–1.
43 Paul Schrader Papers.
44 'Spielberg Speaks About *Close Encounters*' (Interview with Herb

Lightman), *American Cinematographer* 59, no. 1 (January 1978), p. 40.

45 Paul Schrader, *Schrader on Schrader*, ed. Kenneth Jackson (London: Faber & Faber, 2004), pp. 125–6.

46 Telephone conversation, 23 January 2023.

47 Molly Haskell, *Steven Spielberg: A Life in Films* (New Haven, CT: Yale University Press, 2018).

48 In an excellent extended review of the film, especially around its self-reflexive celebration of cinema itself, Garrett Stewart offers this astute comment:

> Roy and his fellow travelers to the unknown embody the artistic drive itself, the compulsive attempt, out of whatever mysterious promptings, to reveal an ideal in pigment or clay – or, of course, celluloid ... a truth that will only be realized, fully visualized by Spielberg's own manipulation of the film medium in the movie's final thunderous annunciation.

(Stewart, 'Close Encounters of the Fourth Kind', *Sight & Sound* 47, no. 3 [Summer 1978], p. 168.)

49 B. H. Fairchild Jr, 'An Event Sociologique: *Close Encounters*', *Journal of Popular Film* 6, no. 4 (1978), p. 343. My friend Caryl Flinn adds insightfully that when Lacombe goes on to say that some UFO witnesses didn't come to the site since they missed the TV broadcast about Devils Tower that was so revealing for Roy Neary (but which he almost missed himself), this is in keeping with the movie's own celebration of its cinematic powers, including over TV perhaps: watching this scene in a movie theatre in 1977, we share in an experience that is more communal – and therefore deemed more consequential – than isolated acts of television viewing. Another friend, Sharrona Pearl, observes additionally that the scene of Roy moving around his living room while his TV relays images of Devils Tower plays with qualities of scale – all to the benefit of cinema's celebration of itself: within the framed large space of film, Roy makes a small-size version of the mountain he is soon to encounter in all its immensity, while the television set – a screen within the movie screen – offers a small-format version of a sublime vision, both real and cinematic together.

50 François Truffaut, 'What Do Critics Dream About?', in *The Films in My Life*, trans. Leonard Mayhew (New York: Da Capo Press, 1985), p. 15. The French original is from 1975 but maybe Fairchild didn't know the reference.

51 Fairchild Jr, 'An Event Sociologique', p. 343.

52 William Flanagan, 'An Encounter with "Close Encounters"', *New York* (7 November 1977), p. 48.

53 Ibid., p. 49.

54 Pauline Kael, 'The Current Cinema: The Greening of the Solar System', *The New Yorker* (28 November 1977), pp. 174–8. For a wild and wacky contrarian view, it is worth quoting in full (as Julie Turnock does in her effects study, *Plastic Reality*, p. 302 *n*50) avant-garde film-maker Kenneth Anger's 'review' of *Close Encounters* soon after the film's release:

Why have I been back to see CLOSE ENCOUNTERS OF THE THIRD KIND six times, braving lines, wait, cold, and four-buck-fifty admission price?

Can it be I love the movie? Listen, I have been back to see Close Encounters of the Third Kind to see if I have been ripped off. I mean *Scorpio Rising* [1964]. The toys, the kid. I mean. LUCIFER RISING [1973–1981]. The saucers. Subject dear to my heart.

Other movies that have ripped off Kenneth Anger. AMERICAN GRAFFITI (music), ELECTRIC GLIDE IN BLUE (theme) I've stayed away from. Not Close Encounters of the Third Kind. I've been back to see it six times.

Then there's the matter of my name (abbreviated) on the track. There it is, *Dolbyized and it sounds just like kenanger* in the burst of static in the start of the Indianapolis control room scene.

Is that punk hustler Spielberg trying to tell me something like: Haw, haw, ripped you off!?!?

(Anger, 'A Short Review of *Close Encounters of the Third Kind*', *Film Comment* 14, no. 1 [January–February 1978], p. 54.)

55 Ursula K. Le Guin, 'Tangents: Film Review', *Parabola* 3, no. 1 (Winter 1978), pp. 92–4.

56 Email to author from Ken Sweeney, 10 November 2022.

57 Ibid.

58 Sayles's script is available online at: <https://ia601207.us.archive.org/6/items/NightSkies/Night%20Skies.pdf> (accessed 11 October 2022).

59 Email to author from Trevor Davis, 17 November 2022.

Image credits

Images from *2001: A Space Odyssey* (Stanley Kubrick, 1968), © Metro-Goldwyn-Mayer, Inc.; *Close Encounters of the Third Kind (Special Edition)* (Steven Spielberg, 1980), EMI Films, Inc./Phillips Production/Columbia Pictures Corporation; *Jaws* (Steven Spielberg, 1975), © Universal Pictures; *Smokey and the Bandit* (Hal Needham, 1977), Rastar Productions/Universal Pictures; *Taxi Driver* (Martin Scorsese, 1976), © Columbia Pictures Industries, Inc.; *Saturday Night Fever* (John Badham, 1977), Paramount Pictures Corporation; *Five Easy Pieces* (Bob Rafelson, 1970), © Five Easy Pieces Productions; *Close Encounters of the Third Kind (Collector's Edition)* (Steven Spielberg, 1998), © Columbia Pictures Industries, Inc.

Credits

Close Encounters of the Third Kind
USA
1977

Written and Directed by
Steven Spielberg
Produced by
Julia Phillips
Michael Phillips

Columbia Pictures in association with EMI
A Julia Phillips & Michael Phillips production

Director of Photography
Vilmos Zsigmond
Director of Photography (Additional American Scenes)
William A. Fraker
Director of Photography (India Sequences)
Douglas Slocombe
Production Designer
Joe Alves
Special Photographic Effects
Douglas Trumbull
Music
John Williams
Film Editor
Michael Kahn
Associate Producer
Clark Paylow
Visual Effects Concepts
Steven Spielberg
Unit Production Manager
Clark Paylow
Additional Directors of Photography
John Alonzo
László Kovács
Technical Advisor
Dr J. Allen Hynek
Set Decorator
Phil Abramson
Realisation of 'Extraterrestrial'
Carlo Rambaldi
Art Director
Dan Lomino
Assistant Director
Chuck Myers
2nd Assistant Director
Jim Bloom
Assistant Film Editors
Geoffrey Rowland
Charles Bornstein
Music Editor
Kenneth Wannberg
Supervising Sound Effects Editor
Frank Warner
Sound Effects Editorial Staff
Richard Oswald
David Horton
Sam Gemette
Gary S. Gerlich
Chet Slomka
Neil Burrow
Production Illustrator
George Jensen
Dolby Sound Supervisor
Steve Katz
Supervising Dialogue Editor
Jack Schrader
Production Sound Mixer
Gene Cantamessa
Music Scoring Mixer
John Neal
Video Technician
'Fast' Eddie Mahler
Camera Operator
Nick McLean
Construction Manager
Bill Parks
Special Mechanical Effects
Roy Arbogast
Dialogue Editorial Staff
Dick Friedman
Assistant Dialogue Staff
Robert A. Reich
Bill Jackson
Technical Dialogue
Colin Cantwell
Re-recording Mixers
Buzz Knudson
Don MacDougall
Robert Glass
Assistant to the Producers
Kendall Cooper
2nd Assistant to the Producers
Judy Bornstein
Assistant to Mr Spielberg
Rick Fields
Production Secretary
Gail Siemers

Production Staff
Janet Healy
Pat Burns
Make-up Supervisor
Bob Westmoreland
Hairdresser
Edie Panda
Casting
Shari Rhodes
Juliette Taylor
Additional Casting
Sally Dennison
Property Master
Sam Gordon
Wardrobe Supervisor
Jim Linn
A.F.I. Intern
Seth Winston
Stunt Co-ordinator
Buddy Joe Hooker
Script Supervision
Charlsie Bryant
Publicity
Al Ebner
Murray Weissman
Pickwick Public Relations
Title Design
Dan Perri
2nd Unit Director of Photography
Steve Poster
Location Auditor
Steve Warner
Location Manager
Joe O'Har
Gaffer
Earl Gilbert
Still Photographers
Pete Sorel
Jim Coe
Pete Turner
Special Photographic Effects Supervised by
Douglas Trumbull
Director of Photography/ Photographic Effects
Richard Yuricich
Matte Artist
Matthew Yuricich
Effects Unit Project Manager
Robert Shepherd
Special Visual Effects Co-ordinator
Larry Robinson
UFO Photography
Dave Stewart
Chief Model Maker
Gregory Jein
Animation Supervisor
Robert Swarthe
Optical Photography
Robert Hall
Matte Photography
Don Jarel
Mother-ship Photography
Dennis Muren
Project Co-ordinator
Mona Thal Benefiel
Camera Operators
Dave Berry
Eugene Eyerly
Maxwell Morgan
Ron Peterson
Eldon Rickman
Technician
Robert Hollister
Assistant Cameramen
David Hardberger
Alan Harding
Bruce Nicholson
Richard Rippel
Scott Squires
Still Photography
Marcia Reid
Model Shop Co-ordinator
J. Richard Dow
Model Makers
Jor Van Kline
Michael McMillen
Kenneth Swenson
Robert Worthington
Camera and Mechanical Design
Don Trumbull (B.G. Engineering)
John Russell
Fries Engineering
Mechanical Special Effects
George Polkinghorne
Electronics Design
Jerry L. Jeffress
Alvah J. Miller
Peter Regla
Dan Slater
Assistant Matte Artist
Rocco Gioffre
Effects Electrician
David Gold
Key Grip
Ray Rich
Laboratory Expeditor
Charles Hinkle
Animator
Harry Moreau
Animation Staff
Carol Boardman
Eleanor Dahlen
Cy Didjurgis

Tom Koester
Bill Millar
Conne Morgan
Production Secretary
Joyce Goldberg
Production Accountant
Peggy Rosson
Project Assistants
Glenn Erickson
Hoyt Yeatman
Editorial Assistant
Joseph A. Ippolito
Transportation
Bill Bethea
Laboratory Technicians
Don Dow
Tom Hollister
Effects Negative Cutter
Barbara Morrison
Special Consultants
Peter Anderson
Larry Albright
Richard Bennett
Ken Ebert
Paul Huston
David M. Jones
Kevin Kelly
Jim Lutes
George Randle
Jeff Shapiro
Rourke Engineering
Colour Consultant
Robert M. McMillian
Special Thanks to
Johnny Mathis
Soundtrack
'Chances Are', words and music by Al Stillman and Robert Allen, published by International Korwin Corp., from the Columbia Records album *Johnny Mathis' All-Time Greatest Hits*; 'When You Wish Upon a Star', words by Ned Washington, music by Leigh Harline, © 1940 Bourne Co.; 'The Square Song', words and music by Joseph Raposo, published by Jonico Music, Inc., courtesy Pickwick International, Inc.; 'Love Song of the Waterfall', words and music by Bob Nolan, Bernard Barnes and Carl Winge, published by Unichappell Music, Inc./Elvis Presley Music, from the United Artists Records album *Love Song of the Waterfall*, sung by Slim Whitman

The Producers Wish to Thank

The Governors and people of Alabama and Wyoming
The Government of India
Kodaly Musical Training Institute, Inc.

Excerpt from *The Ten Commandments* furnished courtesy of Paramount Pictures Corporation, © 1956 by Paramount Pictures Corporation

CAST
Richard Dreyfuss
Roy Neary
François Truffaut
Claude Lacombe
Teri Garr
Ronnie Neary
Melinda Dillon
Jillian Guiler
Bob Balaban
David Laughlin
J. Patrick McNamara
project leader
Warren Kemmerling
Wild Bill
Roberts Blossom
farmer
Philip Dodds
Jean Claude
Cary Guffey
Barry Guiler
Shawn Bishop
Brad Neary
Adrienne Campbell
Silvia Neary
Justin Dreyfuss
Toby Neary
Lance Henriksen
Robert
Merrill Connally
team leader
George DiCenzo
Major Benchley
Amy Douglass
Alexander Lockwood
implantees
Gene Dynarski
Ike
Mary Gafrey
Mrs Harris

Norman Bartold
Ohio tolls
Josef Sommer
Larry Butler
Rev. Michael J. Dyer
as himself
Roger Ernest
highway patrolman
Carl Weathers
military police
F. J. O'Neil
ARP project manager
Phil Dodds
ARP musician
Randy Hermann
returnee 1 Flt 19
Hal Barwood
returnee 2 Flt 19
Matthew Robbins
returnee 3 Flt 19
David Anderson
Richard L. Hawkins
air traffic controllers
Craig Shreeve
Bill Thurman
air traffic
Roy E. Richards
Air East pilot
Gene Rader
hawker
Eumenio Blanco
Daniel Nunez
Chuy Franco
Luis Contreras
federales
James Keane
Dennis McMullen
Cy Young
Tom Howard
radio telescope team
Richard Stuart
truck dispatcher
Bob Westmoreland
load dispatcher
Matt Emery
support leader
Galen Thompson
John Dennis Johnston
Special Forces
John Ewing
dirty tricks 1
Keith Atkinson
dirty tricks 2
Robert Broyles
dirty tricks 3
Kirk Raymond
dirty tricks 4

uncredited
Lewis Abernathy
technician
Bruce Davidson
World War II pilot
Bennett Wayne Dean Sr
scientist
Danyi Deats
alien
Norman Dreyfuss
executive engineer
Ted Henning
power plant technician
Basil Hoffman
Longly
J. Allen Hynek
scientist/returnee
Jenny Inge
alien 1
Monty Jordan
Special Forces
Commander/
helicopter pilot
Shay McLean
speaking child
Dejah Moore
receptionist
Carl Neal
extra
Monty O'Grady
agent
Julia Phillips
UFO watcher at
Crescendo Summit
Murray Pollack
agent
Stephen Powers
UN observer
David Rambow
Special Forces hazmat
soldier
Howard K. Smith
as himself
Bob Westmoreland
returnee

Production Details
35mm
2.39:1
Colour
Dolby
Running time:
135 minutes

Release Details
US theatrical release on
14 December 1978 by
Columbia Pictures
UK theatrical release
on 14 March 1978 by
Columbia-Warner
Distributors